GOODBYE, STATUS QUO

REIMAGINING THE LANDSCAPE OF INNOVATION

DR. JOAN FALLON

Founder & CEO of Curemark

Forefront
BOOKS

To my mom, who recently left the earth but
whose wisdom remains in all of us.

CONTENTS

SECTION 1
THE LANDSCAPE OF CHANGE

SECTION 2
IMPEDIMENTS TO CHANGE

SECTION 3
MAKING CHANGE HAPPEN

FOREWORD

In 2014, my Aunt Joan received the NorthStar Award from Springboard Enterprises at their annual gala for her exceptional entrepreneurial leadership and immense progress in Autism research. Akin to the way in which the North Star shines so eminently in the sky, providing direction to those astray, my aunt has imparted guidance to others.

Although numerous people whom I believed to be more qualified to speak inquired about introducing my aunt, she asked me if I would speak. Being that I was only thirteen at the time, I was not a proficient public speaker; thus, delivering a speech in front of 300 people seemed like a daunting task. Today I find myself in similar uncharted territory—writing the foreword to my aunt's problem-solving book. As a result of this, I thought that it would be appropriate to retell the story that I told in that speech seven years ago—a story of adaption, change, and self-belief.

Some months ago, on a Sunday afternoon, my Aunt Joan and I played a friendly game of one-on-one basketball in my backyard. Aunt Joan, beginning with the ball, drove to the hoop and missed her first shot. Then it was my turn with the ball. I did the famous Pistol Pete two-dribble behind the back and went up for a seventeen-footer . . . swoosh, nothing but net.

2–0—me.

Then it was Aunt Joan's turn with the ball. She went up for a seven-footer and I could not help myself. I stuffed her. I blocked the shot.

Something that you don't know about my Aunt Joan is that she is a real competitor. She won the city of Yonkers foul-shooting championship at thirteen as well as the New York City one-on-one championship in her senior year of high school. She knows the game and has taught it to me.

While these are great basketball accomplishments, what she has taken from those days is an intensity and fire that she brings to everything she does, as well as an understanding that the better those are around you, the better you, too, can be. Thank you, Aunt Joan, for igniting that same competitive fire in me. You are the one who made me always want to get better; you are the one who always makes me better.

This past summer, I had the opportunity to be in a foul-shooting competition at basketball camp. There were 200 kids competing and even more spectators watching. I went to the line. I did my pre-foul-shooting routine and took my first shot. And I missed it.

Everyone was watching and there was all this pressure on me. Then I remembered my Aunt Joan's words that she always said to me, and they rang loudly in my head:

"You can make any shot you want to."

I went on to shoot nineteen of twenty, and I came in second out of those 200 kids.

Now, you may already know that my Aunt Joan is innovative in her own right as she has developed a treatment for Autism. But what you may not know is that my Aunt Joan is an altruistic and resilient individual with an unwavering desire to inspire those around her.

When you are around her, you feel that you, too, can make any shot you want. That inspiration and belief in myself is a gift she gives me every day. This book gives *you*, the reader, that same gift.

—James Edward Fallon

INTRODUCTION
BREAKING THE MOLD

As a female founder in my fifties, I have found that the path to innovation is littered with obstacles. Some of those obstacles are external, like the naysayers who tell you that you are not capable, the noisemakers who drown out every other voice in the room, and the risk that is inevitable in any entrepreneurial venture. However, in my experience, the greatest obstacles often come from within. For me, these internal obstacles ranged from a lack of self-belief, a tendency to be too rigid in the face of changing circumstances, to a failure to take account of other people's needs and perspectives.

As a trained clinician rather than a seasoned business executive, I went from running a practice to being a CEO of a biotech company in what felt like a minute. Making a discovery and wanting to transform that discovery into a business was fraught with obstacles as I built my company. I had to find ways over, around, and beyond obstacles. At certain times throughout my journey as I embrace risk, I have found it useful to observe like a scientist. At other times, I have found it useful to read the field like a Major League Baseball player. And most important, I remind myself to never, ever, lose sight of who I am.

It was evidenced from early childhood that I had three loves in my life:

- Children
- Medicine/Science
- Baseball (or anything with a ball)

My favorite gift of all time was a *real* cardiology stethoscope that my cousin who was in medical school gave me for my tenth birthday. I love children and always have since I was a child. And of course, baseball, which has become a passion of mine. All three of these passions permeate my life even today and are reflected in this book in so many ways. What I find remarkable is that I have been able to integrate all three today in my life in ways I could never have imagined. So whether that is having my company sponsor sensory safe suites for children with Autism and special needs at two Minor League parks where the whole family can watch a baseball game in a safe place for them or being able to speak with a young Major League ballplayer who is struggling to find his mojo, the integration for me is such a joy.

I want this book to speak to anyone who doesn't think that their ideas are valuable or that their lack of experience translates into an inability to become an entrepreneur or changemaker. It's also for those entrepreneurs who do not fit the Silicon Valley stereotype of an entrepreneur, or even their own archetype of a changemaker. This book is for anyone who has been told any of the following: you are not male, you are not young enough, you are not smart enough, experienced enough, white enough, or from the right school. If that is you, I want you to know that regardless of where you come from, you *can* change the world—if you are willing to first change yourself.

Changing the world by starting a company and solving problems may sound like an audacious goal. It is my experience that every time a company builds empathy into its working methods, a college makes an effort to attract first-generation college students, a woman or a person of color takes ownership of their ideas by filing a patent, or a company hires a diverse workforce and finds a great way to integrate that workforce—every single action of this kind makes a difference in the world.

This book is divided into three sections: The Landscape of Change, Impediments to Change, and Making Change Happen. It follows a broad flow from observations on the wider world to your immediate surroundings, to the inner world of an entrepreneur or changemaker. Naturally I hope you will read every chapter from beginning to end, but I'm sure that some of you will jump to the chapters that seem most relevant to you. I've written this book in such a way that you can do that too.

While reading through this book, please keep in mind that if you wish to make change in the world in whatever way you see fit, it will always start with a willingness for self-change, a willingness to bend in the wake of upheaval around you, and the notion that learning is not a singular event but rather, a lifelong one.

When you finish reading, I hope that you will share my view that founders and changemakers benefit from having a blend of self-belief, a willingness to change, a commitment to learning, and a whole bunch of grit and grace under fire. You don't need to be the bully in the room to make an impact. If you want to innovate and make a difference in the world, do it your way—not anyone else's.

SECTION 1

THE LANDSCAPE OF CHANGE

HOW BROADENING OUR PERSPECTIVE HELPS US TO SOLVE PROBLEMS

CHAPTER 1

INNOVATE WITH EMPATHY

Through creativity and innovation, we transformed
barren deserts into flourishing fields and pioneered
new frontiers in science and technology.
—SHIMON PERES (PRESIDENT OF ISRAEL, 2007–2014)

For the past twelve years, a dear friend and I have made a pact to spend a week or two during the summer taking classes or participating in something that has impact and can help us better understand the world we live in with an eye toward making it a better place. While living on opposite coasts 3,000 miles apart, we have found a common bond in our summer learning experiences. We've studied leadership at the Harvard Kennedy School (HKS) of Government and entrepreneurship at the London School of Economics, and we have attended the Resnick Aspen Action Forum at the Aspen Institute, among other adventures.

At HKS we learned that leadership is about solving problems. Great leaders solve problems by harvesting ideas and motivating others to act, thereby creating change. In addition to the ones mentioned, one of the most profound summer experiences we had was at the design school at Stanford (commonly referred to as the "d.school"), where we learned to identify problems and work on ways to solve them through design thinking. Design thinking gives a solution-focused approach to problem-solving using known steps that can help not only to solve a problem, but solve the *correct* problem.

Stanford's d.school sees its mission in the following way:

To help people unlock their creative abilities and apply them to the world. It reflects our foundational belief that design should be accessible to all, and that everyone is creative.

We believe design can help create the world we wish for. Design can activate us as creators and change the way we see ourselves and others. Design is filled with optimism, hope, and the joy that comes from making things change by making things real. We believe that diversity leads to better design and opens up a greater range of creative possibilities.[1]

We attended the d.school's "Design Thinking Bootcamp," where for a week we learned the design thinking process and then worked on real-world problems. During that week we teamed up with people from all over the world. Some of us had entrepreneurial backgrounds and worked at or ran small businesses; others had large corporate experience or came out of finance or other business sectors. I had already founded Curemark, and I was hungry for ways to look at problems differently.

The d.school way of solving problems isn't to sit around a room and discuss a theoretical problem. Rather, it involves going into the field and talking to real people about their experiences and things they see as helpful or issues that present as problems for them. Because the design thinking model involves active participation to understand a problem, it differed from my previous ways of looking at things as generally patients brought problems to me, and while I may have examined them and asked questions, I generally tapped into my "learnings" for answers.

Design thinking as envisaged by the d.school has eight core elements:

Adapted from d.school

Each step in this process follows the previous one. What initially was striking to me was the fact that if these are performed out of order, either the problem being solved or the ultimate solution may not be the right one or best one.

Let's look at these steps:

Uncertainty—Approach a problem where the solution is not obvious or the actual problem is not obvious.

Empathize—Put yourself in someone else's shoes. Understand other worldviews, feelings, and needs.

Synthesize—Gather data about the problems that need to be solved, and then put that data together to come up with potential solutions.

Ideate—Put together various ideas about what problems to solve and discuss ideas.

Stakeholders—Determine who the stakeholders are and get the ideas to them about what to solve.

Prototype—Make a working model of how a problem could be solved. Can involve an actual physical model.

Testing and Feedback—Take the prototype and put it into mock action to gain feedback about what does and does not work.

Design the Product—When the feedback and testing are done, design an actual working model for full implementation.

As part of our weeklong assignment at the bootcamp, we were tasked to spend time at the Jet Blue terminal in San Francisco International Airport (SFO) and uncover problems that existed there. Jet Blue was sincerely interested in making their terminal experience a friendly and positive one, not only for their passengers and customers but also for those who worked in their terminal. We interviewed passengers, store vendors, airline staff, and even TSA agents to identify what *they* perceived as problems with the airport. Once we had identified some problems, we went back to Stanford and spend the rest of the week solving one of them.

When you think of an airport, many, many problems come to mind: long lines, wait times, and crowded terminals, just for starters. I assumed that wait times and flight delays must be the number one problem. Surely that must be the biggest source of stress for all air travelers. No one likes hanging around an airport terminal, right? So you might set out to solve that problem with better scheduling, or maybe you would create more effective notification systems to bring passengers to the airport in time to catch their planes—but without a long wait.

Alas, I was wrong. It turned out that wait time was not the number one problem at this airport at all. The nature of the experience at the terminal was more stressful for passengers. More than anything else, travelers told us that they were frustrated by the lack of amenities available at the airport that they could use during a wait. Passengers were generally quite understanding about weather delays and mechanical failures. What riled them were the things that were lacking: water fountains, electronics charging stations, places for children to play, a wider range of food options, dog parks for service animals, and rooms to nurse infants. All of these needs were far more problematic than wait times.

Looking back at the d.school model for design thinking, I believe that no piece of this model is more important than the first two elements: uncertainty and empathize. In order to remain open to discover a problem and then remedy it, you must remain for a time in uncertainty. (We will discuss uncertainty in more detail in Chapter 8.) Solutions are often not clear-cut, and the correct path to a solution emerges from the uncertainty and ambiguity that come from being patient and subscribing to a process such as design thinking.

Empathy (which we will discuss later in this chapter) is probably the single most important part of this process. Empathy is the experience of putting oneself in someone else's shoes to have the best understanding of another's circumstance as is humanly possible. Empathy is having a clear understanding of human needs—what someone other than yourself needs or experiences or feels. Without empathy, we cannot effectuate change and fix problems. With empathy, we can solve real problems. There is no replacing this step. While some believe that augmented reality and artificial intelligence can replicate or ultimately mimic an experience and therefore create empathy, I am not yet convinced.

Today as you walk through the terminals in many major airports (including SFO), you will see nursing rooms and pods, service dog relief areas, and passengers using apps to order meals delivered to their gates. These are real solutions to the real problems we found in our d.school journey. Jet Blue was a d.school partner and was the first to implement many of these amenities.

A common misconception is that leaders are the people with the most charisma in the room or the ones who make the boldest business moves. Some see leadership as the ability to organize or mobilize people for a cause. While these qualities may indeed be found in some leaders, the greatest distinguishing feature that sets great leaders apart is that they *solve problems*.

Put simply—true leaders change society and the world with new ideas. With that said, not all leaders excel at leading people; some are thought leaders and others design solutions or products that solve problems. Was Steve Jobs a great leader of people? Maybe not, but he certainly was a *thought leader* and an outstanding innovator. His genius lay in giving you what you didn't yet know you needed, solving a problem you didn't know you had as opposed to solving a problem you know you have. For example, Steve Jobs gave us the iPhone, a unique tool that we didn't know we needed and yet now many of us cannot do without. I once heard Larry Summer, the former president of Harvard, on a stage ask and answer a question: "If someone gave me easy access to all of the information contained in the libraries at Harvard or this iPhone, I would choose the iPhone."

Martin Luther King Jr. and Mahatma Gandhi, two great leaders, led through peaceful protest as they fought discrimination and unfair treatment of people living in poverty and people of color. In the following pages, you will see how each saw an insidious disparity that ran deep and wide in cultures that were ingrained with white elitism and white supremacy. They were not leaders like Steve Jobs, an inventor who anticipated what we needed. (And just think about what both King and Gandhi could have done with an iPhone.) Neither completed the task of undoing discriminatory practices, but MLK saw the passage of the Voting Rights Act, and Gandhi, the ultimate freedom of his beloved India.

Abraham Lincoln inherited a country torn over the issue of slavery. He spoke of a house divided. In April 1864 he gave an address in Baltimore where he stated: "The world has never had a good definition of the word liberty, and the American people, just now, are much in need of one. We all declare for liberty; but in using the same *word* we do not all mean the same *thing.*" (emphasis mine) His views on slavery morphed over time; he understood that slavery was morally wrong, but he also recognized that freedom and liberty in the days in which he lived did not mean equality. Although he issued the Emancipation Proclamation, he also knew that there were economic and logistical issues of what the freed slaves were entitled to and where they could live and make a living. Like Gandhi and MLK, Lincoln began to solve a deep-seated problem that in many ways still exists, and which many of today's leaders are still chipping away at it, albeit slowly. In recent years, the social movement Black Lives Matter has brought the continued deep racial divide into our living rooms. We must understand our past and the fact that deep racial bias still exists in our world. But with awareness comes change.

Ghandi, Lincoln, and MLK are just three examples of leaders who came into a place in history where their leadership solved problems. In all three examples, they did not solve the problem fully, but they looked around and realized that there was some immediacy to what needed to change. In each case, their empathy and their willingness to live in uncertainty were clearly apparent, and each moved us to new levels of realization and a betterment of humankind. All three lost their lives as a result of their attempts to change the world and to bring equality to the forefront.

The people most likely to change the world are the ones who observe the need for it most keenly, who put themselves in other people's places, and who understand what others feel or think. Where and how having empathy can help with leadership. Following are three precepts to keep in mind as you attempt to solve problems, effectuate change, and lead others.

1. CHANGE THE WAY YOU SEE THE WORLD

If you go into a dark movie theatre, once you've found your seat, you'll look around for the exit signs. If you drive along a road where a landslide has littered the way with boulders and tree roots, you'll seek alternative routes or the most efficient way to navigate that road. Tunnel vision is your enemy in that dark room or on that hazardous road. "Looking around"—scanning your environment to identify the best path through it—is of paramount importance.

As an entrepreneur or changemaker, finding the way to the next step is *the* most essential component of change.

Wherever you are sitting or standing right now, look around you. Scan your physical environment and consider where change is needed. Is it too hot? Or maybe too cluttered? Is the meeting in the conference room next door distracting? Can you smell someone's lunch being heated in the microwave?

See things how they really are. See it all.

When people look around them, they most often do it with a prejudicial eye. They start out believing they already know what is important to see. The reality is that everything is important to look at, not just the things you have already decided are important.

My company, Curemark, develops treatments for unmet medical needs, and the first product in development is to treat Autism. We had run multiple clinical trials and the pandemic hit while children were still in a trial. The need for sameness is one of the hallmarks of children with Autism, and the pandemic suddenly forced them to change everything about their routine. They were no longer going to school, yet school is where most of their ancillary services such as speech therapy, occupational therapy, and socialization classes take place. They were home with siblings and parents, no longer seeing their teachers in person or having the benefit of their "shadow" or aide whom they often depend upon. Everything for these children had changed, so how does one look at their behavior pre-COVID and post-COVID? How does their environment alter their well-being? How does a sudden change in their lives register in their behavior? They are home all the time . . . so what has changed for them? Just about everything!

I don't think anyone could have seen pre-pandemic the level of food insufficiency we saw in the U.S. or the inability for many women to be gainfully employed when they have three or four children at home who needed to be homeschooled. Even as the lockdown began, we did not foresee things such as a lack of broadband or the inability of a school district to pivot to online learning. By actively employing empathy and an understanding of what others are experiencing, society began to address some of these problems in real time while others have yet to be solved.

2. OBSERVATION REQUIRES EMPATHY

The Harvard Kennedy School has an excellent summer program, and my friend from San Francisco and I attended sessions on leadership there one summer. During that week we met a gentleman teaching in the program. He introduced himself as Jamil Mahuad, the former president of Ecuador.

Jamil is a humble, authentic man who taught us something important. While it is a story that's been told many times and is part of history, having the former president himself tell us the story of his presidency was very meaningful. Originally a well-respected mayor of Quito, he was beloved by the people and ultimately elected president. He told our class the story of how his greatest ambition when he governed Ecuador as president was to end a border dispute between his country and Peru that dated back two centuries. At one time, Ecuador reached beyond the Andes mountain range to the Amazon river, including the Amazonian Basin. In the 19th century, Ecuador and Peru battled over the land as treaties were signed and disputed and conflicts were sparked, resolved, and restarted again. Mahuad was determined to be the one to claim that fertile piece of land, once and for all. Mahuad wanted to be the one to settle this historic dispute. It didn't quite turn out as he had hoped.

At that time in 1998, Ecuador was going through a terrible recession. Oil, which was its main export, dropped in price to $20 a barrel. Floods battered the nation, causing $2.6 billion in damage. Inflation was pushing 50 percent, the highest in Latin America, and austerity measures hit the already impoverished Ecuadorian people hard. The Ecuadorians staged a two-day nationwide strike to protest the government's mismanagement.

All this time Mahuad was obsessed about claiming this little piece of land. Nothing else truly grabbed his attention. President Mahuad chased Fujimori (the president of Peru July 28, 1990, to November 22, 2000) all over the world, all the time ignoring what was taking place in his country or how much his people were suffering. After a week of demonstrations and a military revolt, protesters took over the legislative palace, forcing Mahuad to resign and to flee into exile.

Mahuad had become blind to the needs of his people and what was going on in his country. Had he not been off chasing President Fujimori of Peru and a piece of land, he would have observed that the Ecuadorian people were hungry and desperate for change.

President Mahuad did succeed in one thing: a resolution with Peru allowed Ecuador to be granted an area of one square kilometer of land—just one square kilometer—less than one-third the size of New York City's Central Park.

This story truly struck me and stayed with me because of the profound mismatch in attention and the lack of empathy Mahuad exhibited toward his people. His fixation on a problem that was not the important one to solve led to his own ouster and exile. Had he just looked around and seen the suffering of his people and exercised empathy toward them, he could have helped them by solving the country's greater problem.

3. YOU MUST FIND TRUE EMPATHY

Of all the people in recent times who have brought empathy to the forefront of our thoughts and conversations, Dr. Brené Brown stands apart. She has spent more than two decades studying courage, vulnerability, shame, and empathy. Through her TED talks, books, and podcasts, she shows us that both empathy and vulnerability are key attributes for making successful relationships and finding connection with others. She often states, "Rarely can a response make something better. What makes something better is connection."

In her book *I Thought It Was Just Me (But It Isn't)*, Brown refers to nursing scholar Theresa Wiseman's four attributes of empathy:[2]

- **To be able to see the world as others see it.** This requires putting your own "stuff" aside to see the situation through your loved one's eyes.

- **To be nonjudgmental.** Judgement of another person's situation discounts their experience and is an attempt to protect ourselves from the pain of the situation.
- **To understand another person's feelings.** We have to be in touch with our own feelings in order to understand someone else's. Again, this requires putting your own "stuff" aside to focus on your loved one.
- **To communicate your understanding of that person's feelings.** Rather than saying, "At least you . . ." or "It could be worse . . ." try, "I've been there, and that really hurts."

With empathy one learns what it feels like to be heard and accepted. We must first grasp our own vulnerability through courage and self-acceptance in order to exercise that empathy muscle. Self-acceptance, of course, only comes with the ability to deal with one's shame—and that's the subject of the next chapter.

Empathy is often confused with or used interchangeably with sympathy. They are two very different responses, two very different positions. Empathy places you in the position, in the proverbial shoes, in the mindset and feelings of *others*. Sympathy is what *you* feel about the circumstances that others are going through.

Empathy is an equal force, a magnet that draws us together. It creates connection because you are standing in someone else's position. When you walk in empathy, you have to get into another person's shoes. You try to be them, in the most real way you can.

Sympathy sets up an unequal moment. "I feel *this* because you are going through *that*." Sympathy puts a wedge between people and stands in the way of true connection.

I believe that one of the issues that hangs in the air with race relationships in this country is that white people often cannot find the space of empathy with their Black and Brown neighbors.

Implicit bias has buried our ability to be vulnerable and to really look at the experiences of people of color both historically and in the current moment. Most of the time we cannot even see or hear their experiences, let alone respond to it—while all the time inequity runs rampant.

During the pandemic I was invited to a women's Friday night Zoom gathering by someone I know well, who thought I would enjoy the conversation with these women at the end of the week. The call was populated with women I did not know, but many of them were the spouses of major sports stars, every name well known in the sports world. Each of these women, some of color and some not, was married to an athlete of color. To hear their concern for their children, especially their male children, was an amazing experience for me.

Besides the concern for their male children being stopped by the police while driving and ending up in some type of incident, one mother expressed concern when her children went to other people's homes.

She said to her children, "When you go to your friend's home, make sure you go with him if he leaves the room."

Now, her children were probably eight and twelve.

"What do you mean, Mom?"

"If Johnny leaves the room for some reason, you must go with him. Don't let him leave you alone in a room without him."

"Huuuuh? Why?"

"White people think that Black people steal, and I don't want you accused of stealing something."

Now, these were children of a mega sports star. But what struck me beyond the words their mom uttered was the sound of her voice when she spoke. She was deeply concerned and worried that her children would be out in the world and be falsely accused with no defense because they were Black. Her voice broke the whole time she was speaking. And she was not the only mom on this call to utter similar things. It made me know that while my mind can understand, my empathy was triggered when I heard the fear in her voice. I imagined being in her shoes and being fearful for my children because they are Black. Her *fear* was palpable and real.

Having empathy allows one to really feel someone else's pain or fear. Without empathy, there are few deep understandings that we can accomplish in our lives with respect to others. Without empathy we are missing the world outside of our own.

Having empathy in our personal lives as well as in our business lives allows us to work smarter, create better solutions, and to make our workplace significantly better for all.

Entrepreneurs often ask me how I have been able to create solutions and have a work environment that has diversity as well as inclusion. We will see later in this text how important inclusion is. Here are some insights with respect to the importance of empathy.

1. Empathy helps you determine what problem to solve.
2. Empathy allows you to solve the problem by uncovering it from the inside—from the point of view of those who will utilize your solution.
3. Empathy expands your vision for your company or product.

Not long ago, I agreed to invest in a company run by a great young man, the son of a colleague of mine. His company was in the business of aggregating video clips to salute a loved one for a birthday, anniversary, or other occasion. It was a lovely idea; you can imagine an elderly grandparent being overwhelmed by such a thoughtful gift from his family. I met with this young man, and we talked through the whole idea. He spoke about how an elderly grandparent in the hospital could receive one of these videos.

"How would my grandfather play the video if he was in a hospital bed, say, and not at home?" I asked him.

He looked at me blankly. "Uh—you'd hand him a USB/ memory stick?"

"So, my grandfather will have a laptop with him in the ICU able to plug in that USB stick?"

"Um . . . ."

"You need to source a bunch of cheap portable video players and make that part of the product," I told him.

This wasn't a conversation about a lack of technology—it was a conversation about a lack of empathy. Put yourself in someone else's shoes to see them using the product you have created. What do they need to use it? What does it do for them?

Gleefully they have become a great company providing an amazing service and have individual playable cards where the video is embedded into, for example, a birthday card. It is because the founder could pivot; he listened and did it right.

In 1990, I was sent on a mission to Romania to assess the children in the orphanages there. Nicolea Ceausescu was the communist dictator whose rule reached every aspect of Romanian society. Early in his tenure he outlawed abortion and made divorce difficult. He rewarded families who had large numbers of children by granting them special designations with special "perks." As a result of this doctrine, Romania began to have an overflow of children, some of whom had simple problems, but which could not be attended to by the family. For example, a child born into a farming family needed to be a functional part of the working family. If the child had strabismus (crossed eyes), they required surgery that was unavailable to them, and the child became a burden. A condition that's corrected every day in the U.S. became a lifelong disability for these Romanian children. The state opened orphanages where parents could place these children, and as long as they were visited at least once a year by their family, they were not eligible for adoption.

This led to overcrowded orphanages, where in many cases three or four children, aged one to seven, shared one crib. It was hard to believe what I saw there. The farther away from the capital of Bucharest the orphanage was located, the worse the conditions and the sicker the children. I recall one orphanage that was located next to a mental hospital; the children often mimicked the behaviors they saw in the courtyard of the mental hospital, which was separated from them only by a wire fence.

It was eye-opening for me, and the lack of care—despite all the people there trying to help—was amazing. Before I went, I asked what was needed, what I could bring, and I was told, bring syringes. I brought 2,000 syringes with me. I met a dentist who volunteered with the kids in the orphanages one day a month whose gratitude for these syringes went beyond words. She told me she only had one glass syringe that she would clean between seeing patients, and the disposable syringes I brought would be very helpful to her.

One day, many years later, I was lecturing about pediatric development in a large auditorium. I was speaking about these kids and their conditions. A doctor in the audience raised her hand to ask a question. "I was in an orphanage in Africa where there was war, and I spent some real time there," she said. "What, to you, was the most distinguishing feature of the orphanage? What struck you the most?" Before I could answer she said, "After all these many years I still have never encountered anything like the smell." As I stood there I was immediately brought back to the odor of the orphanages. It is one that I have never experienced before or since. The smell was a mixture of old dried blood, urine, and feces mixed with chlorine and the "slop" that was fed to the children, which was crusted over the cribs and the tables. A tart, sweet, pungent, acerbic, putrid smell that is unforgettable.

Having had this opportunity and experiences with the orphanages in Romania gave me a complete appreciation for the neglect and bullying an entire nation can produce. Understanding what these children went through, how people reacted to them, and the needs that they had for simple things that we take for granted in our lives was something that changed my life.

Exercising empathy is so important in our personal and professional lives as we seek to solve problems and become leaders.

> The distinguishing feature that sets great leaders apart is that they solve problems. They do it by harvesting ideas and motivating people to act, thereby creating real change that solves real problems.
>
> Exercising empathy can help solve the real and important problems and result in great leadership.

CHAPTER 2

TAKE A GLOBAL VIEW

Don't let one cloud obliterate the whole sky.

—Anaïs Nin, Author

Often when we talk about innovation, we talk about it in terms of "vision." This is no accident. We can learn a great deal about innovation from the physiology of sight.

As a changemaker or entrepreneur, you've probably been told one (or all!) of the following things, many times over:

"Have a vision for your company."

"Focus on the task in front of you."

"Don't get distracted."

"Keep your eyes on the prize."

"Focus, focus, focus."

I'm not going to tell you that these things are wrong. But while focus is a huge part of innovating and creating change, seeing the entire landscape is equally important. Seeing the full vista—what lies ahead, what is around you, and what is right in front of you—allows entrepreneurs to avoid land mines. With this wider perspective, you will find that you are able to walk around the "boulders" or obstacles that come up in your journey. Without perspective, you are more likely to stumble and fall when you misjudge the location or the magnitude of the obstacle in your path.

Let's look at two "vision scenarios." In the first, a person is approaching a "playing field" with the benefit of perspective. Big and small, the obstacles are all visible.

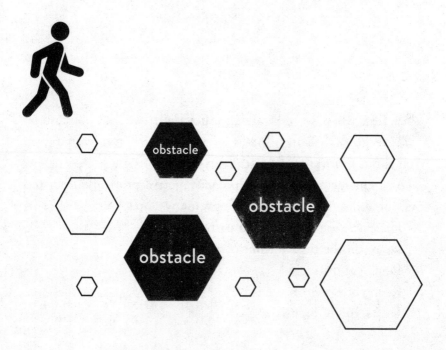

In the second scenario, the person is too close to the obstacles to see a way around them and to find a path forward.

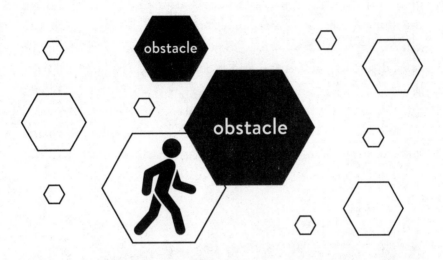

Perspective is achieved through maintaining some distance to the obstacles. It is defined by your relative position to the path ahead of you and where you are at any moment in your journey.

As we look around us, our eyes move about three times per second, presenting us with an ever-changing collage of real-world scenes.[3] As we look at these scenes, we see innumerable objects. Yet remarkably, despite this bombardment of information, we can recognize the "gist" of a scene, making sense of the whole. This *scene gist recognition* is important because it affects our cognitive processes. How can you view a scene and understand it within the first tenth of a second, easily distinguishing between an office versus a parking lot versus a street? And then decide which people and objects to attend to, and which to ignore?

Psychologists Adam Larson and Lester Loschky researched this very question, recruiting 100 undergraduates from Kansas State University to analyze how different parts of their vision contributed to their scene gist recognition.[4] Larson and Loschky showed the students scenes in two experimental conditions, which you can see below. The "Window" view is like a porthole, showing the central portion of a scene and blocking out peripheral information. The "Scotoma" (or peripheral) view is the reverse; it blocks out the central portion and shows only the periphery. The word *scotoma* is a term that has come to mean "blind spot." In medicine, it refers to an area of vision where visual acuity is either diminished or absent.

Window   Scotoma

After analyzing the results, the research team found that peripheral vision is more useful for recognizing the gist of a scene than central vision is. With the focused Window/central view, far less is revealed than with the Scotoma/peripheral view, where a great deal is seen. While it is true that our central vision enables us to see greater detail, our peripheral vision gives us a far greater ability to "get" what is happening in a particular visual field.

There is great interest today in the science of visual acuity as a way of enhancing performance, especially in sports. Many professional sports teams now employ visual therapists and perform extensive vision testing on their athletes. They benefit from studies like the one I described conducted by Kansas State, measuring the level of visual accuracy in central (Window) vision versus peripheral (Scotoma) vision. Players who use their peripheral vision are able to detect motion more effectively and act more swiftly. In sports such as baseball or tennis when a player has to hit a ball moving at 100 mph or more, or in football when a player must block someone who is approaching from the side, peripheral vision can be enormously helpful.

Elite athletes must have not only excellent physical condition and sport-specific skills, they must also have superior visual skills.[5] Field sports such as football and baseball call for a constant balance of central focus, peripheral awareness, and rapid reaction to the ball and to other players. A British study of soccer players found that they had stronger peripheral visual processing skills than central skills. The researchers attributed this fact to more valuable strategic information being gained through observing field movement versus observing ball movement alone.

I grew up in the arcade era, and one of my greatest joys as a kid was to go to Playland in Rye, New York, by the Long Island Sound, and play arcade games to my heart's content. Whac-A-Mole was my favorite. For those of you who are uninitiated in the delights of arcade games, when playing Whac-A-Mole, a player takes a large, soft mallet and uses it to hit mechanical moles that pop up out of five or more holes in a cabinet that stands about waist high. The object of the game is to hit as many moles as possible during a certain time. The moles disappear quickly, so it's quite a test of reflexes and concentration—but also of peripheral vision. The best way to hit each mole is to use your peripheral vision to survey the "landscape of the moles" and determine where the next one will emerge. Looking directly at the board narrows your perceived landscape, rendering you less able to react to the popping moles.

It's not just elite athletes who enjoy the benefit of peripheral vision—arcade game fans score big, too, when they survey the whole scene.

I like to compare the Whac-A-Mole board to the landscape of an entrepreneurial journey—and indeed, a life journey. As you walk forward, it is important to see the whole landscape. Don't get stuck staring up close at that boulder in your way but maintain enough distance to avoid the obstacles so you can keep moving forward. Having the best scene gist view will help you navigate the terrain in front of you. You could say that this gives you a broader view of the "mole landscape" so you can predict more accurately where the next one will pop up. For instance, thinking about tomorrow while also focusing on today will allow you to see the greatest span of the landscape, thereby reducing the likelihood of stumbling on a land mine.

In the corporate world, you don't want to turn away from your goal completely; you just want to make sure that you also have a view of the wider terrain. That may simply require a tweak to your posture, tilting your head a little bit to get a fresh view. Rosabeth Moss Kanter is the Ernest L. Arbuckle Professor of Business Administration at Harvard Business School and author of *Think Outside the Building: How Advanced Leaders Can Change the World One Smart Innovation at a Time*. In her book she describes how important it is for leaders to step outside the building where they work, step outside their silo, and step outside their own thinking in order to innovate and see things differently.

In a recent podcast sponsored by the *Harvard Business Review*, Professor Kanter explained: "Oh, if you step outside, I mean, first of all, you see the world differently. There are many executives and managers who are insulated. They live in little bubbles."[6] She went on to describe why some "advanced leaders," as she calls them, are successful. "These are all people willing to go to new places. They have curiosity. It helps to be at different ends of life: either earlier in your career before the demands of family are so great, or a little later in your career when you've already made it to high levels and your kids are grown. That helps to have the time, but really what they have in common is their values, their desire to make a difference, and the curiosity to learn about the world. Plus, I guess, a feeling that they can do it."

As leaders and change agents, if we only think of what is right in front of our faces, we can't imagine all the pitfalls and problems—nor, for that matter, all the wonder and beauty—that lie just outside our central field of vision. If we concentrate only on what is directly in front of us, we will have an intense view of the details but we will not have a wider vision or the full scene gist view. Additionally, we will not be prompted by new experiences, new people, or new places to innovate in ways that are available to us if we look outside and beyond what is in front of us—or as Professor Kantor puts it, "Outside the building."

I have experienced this myself many times in my career. Over ten years ago, very early in my biotech career, I got a call from our head of manufacturing while I was out of town.

"Joan, we've got a problem with our latest batches," he told me.

"What kind of problem?" I asked

"Well, the packager just called to tell me there are clumps in the material."

"Okay," I said. "I'll be in the office tomorrow. You go to the plant in New Jersey, pick up a clump, and bring it in so we can take a look at it together."

I flew home that evening and went into the office the next morning. The manufacturing head called me around noon. "I can't bring the clump back," he tells me.

"Why not?" I ask.

"The whole output has congealed. It's all one solid clump."

"Okay, come into the office and we'll figure this out."

The whole team sat down to work the problem. None of us had any idea why the material was clumping this way now, when it had never been a problem before.

After circling around for a while, I said, "Okay, call up the manufacturing plant and tell them we're coming over on Tuesday. I want the whole team in there to figure this out."

So that's what we did. All of us went to the plant and sat down with the manufacturing team, and I asked them to talk me through the whole process, every step, one by one.

The packaging plant manager described in detail the entire process, but still, no one had any clue why the "clumping" occurred. All around the table I could see people shaking their heads, perplexed that something had gone wrong—but we couldn't put our finger on what that change was.

After working around various explanations and getting nowhere, I asked the plant manager, "Did you do anything different with this batch? We never had this problem before."

"Well, we introduced foil bagging into the process; we thought it would be a good idea."

"So when you manufacture this stuff, how hot does it get in the process?" I asked.

"About 500 degrees Fahrenheit."

"So did you wait to put the material into the bags after it cooled down?" I asked.

"No."

"So you took extremely hot material and put it in foil bags before it cooled down? What did you expect to happen?" It melted and congealed.

No one had thought the process through. They thought only in specific steps. We all learned something very valuable.

If you don't step back and look at the whole picture, from periphery to center and out again, you can miss things. All of the manufacturing people on both teams were too close to the issue to figure it out.

Especially in a new venture or a start-up, when the founder has eyes on the central part, someone else must look at the periphery. You may even have many eyes on the central piece, but always, *always* give someone the job of looking more widely. I cannot emphasize how important it is for the leader to look outside as well.

Even when you're working at a furious pace to hit a launch date or prepare your business plan for investors, take time to look at potential obstacles or competitive challenges, even if they seem far-fetched or far away. Looking ahead and around will help keep your company out of crisis mode.

As leaders and changemakers, if we only think of what is right in front of our faces, we can't imagine all the pitfalls and problems—nor for that matter, all the wonder and beauty—that lie just outside our central field of vision. If we concentrate only on what is directly in front of us, we will have an intense view of the details, but we will not have a wider vision or the full scene gist view needed to make change.

CHAPTER 3

EMBRACE DISSENT

I find that because of modern technological evolution and our global economy, and as a result of the great increase in population, our world has greatly changed: it has become much smaller. However, our perceptions have not evolved at the same pace; we continue to cling to old national demarcations and the old feelings of "us" and "them."

—His Holiness the 14th Dalai Lama

Leaders, innovators, and changemakers must look widely not only by exercising their own observational skills but by drawing around them the most diverse leadership group possible. In a word: *talent.* As the world becomes increasingly globally connected, diversity of thought and the need for understanding other cultures and mores become imperatives to run a global business. Diversity of thought will bring with it new concepts and thoughts that may vary or diverge significantly from yours. Being challenged and listening to others is key to being successful.

A few years ago, I had the honor of hearing Christine Lagarde, the president of the European Central Bank, speak on the future of finance and seats of power. Lagarde is an enormously accomplished woman; as well as being the former head of the International Monetary Fund (IMF), she is France's former Minister of State for Foreign Trade and former Finance Minister. In her presentation, she talked about the world changing centers of power in a way I had never heard it described before. Countries were no longer going to hold all the influence, she said; seats of power could be cities, or companies, or other organizations, such as NGOs. Lagarde argued that these changes would shape the future.

When I reflected on her remarks afterward, it occurred to me that for centuries, power has been organized around land masses, and wars have been (and continue to be) fought over the borders of those land masses. In many cases, wars are fought over what is contained in those land masses: oil, natural resources, and other valuable assets. Since so much of the world's economy has shifted to a cyber and digital economy and will continue to shift in that direction, land masses and borders are becoming less relevant over time. While coal and oil still dominate in the "old economy," and the scarcity of certain raw materials, such as rare earth elements, will continue to be important, other assets such as digital infrastructure and data will dominate in the "new economy."

Just imagine—no longer will land masses and borders define seats of power. Nations will not be the only category of influence. Struggles over a patch of land, say, on the border of Ecuador and Peru, may no longer be consequential.

"The world is global." Perhaps that has become a cliché, but it's no less true. As the Dalai Lama puts it, our world has "become much smaller." One obvious example is the way we travel with ease from one hemisphere to the other. But globalization is about far more than passenger flights. Globalization allows for nearly instant communication, conveyance of ideas, and implementation of plans—not just locally, but well beyond the vicinity where we live and work. Our world is smaller not only because we can traverse it so much more easily and quickly, but because trade brings goods from one hemisphere to another. We play sports in the same arena with people of vastly different cultures, and we are exposed to ideas that a century ago—perhaps even a decade ago—would have been entirely invisible to us.

Geography no longer limits our interactions. Where once power was defined and aggregated by location—into cities, provinces, nations, regions—that is no longer the case. Taking the place of geographically defined seats of power are tech monoliths such as Apple and banking goliaths such as JPMorgan Chase. We have clearly seen the importance of the World Health Organization (WHO) during the COVID-19 pandemic. The top ten most powerful public companies in the world have a combined asset value of close to 24 trillion dollars compared to the world GDP of approximately $92 trillion.[7] Even some of the largest nongovernmental organizations (NGOs) in the world wield budgets that far surpass some nations' GDPs. You might be surprised to know that the world's largest NGO is an organization called the Bangladesh Rural Advancement Committee (BRAC), which works to alleviate poverty, illiteracy, disease, and social injustice. In 2017 BRAC disbursed U.S. $3.82 billion in loans and reached 110 million people through its services.[8] That's an influential organization.

If globalization is what we have moving forward, we must adapt to the times to effectuate change and to accept the changes that have been thrust upon us.

We now recognize that diversity inside communities, educational institutions, and corporations allow a richer environment. Differing points of view and bringing together various skill sets and talents make a company, school, community, and nation more nimble, stronger, and richer.

Dissent, which can be characterized as a difference of opinion from either prevailing views and opinions or from current policy, adds to the richness of a conversation. It is why for so many years the two-party system of democracy has worked so well in the U.S. In the case of our democracy, the majority party often listened to and incorporated the minority party's opinions and viewpoints. Today, of course, a partisan lack of listening has hurt our democracy but that is a subject for another book. Suffice it to say that differing opinions add tremendously to ultimate decisions.

Let's briefly look at how diversity that surrounds an idea and its potential genesis impact that idea. If you live in a world—or an organization—that lacks diversity, the context that surrounds an idea may look like the following:

X = YES

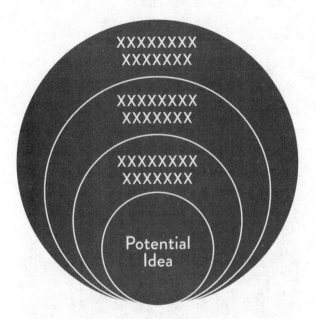

If all of the layers of people and organization that surround an idea lack diversity, and everyone and everything is saying "Yes," the consensus is YES. Of course, this *could* occur when there is diversity, but it's unlikely.

If you surround an idea with people and organizations that are more diverse, the idea itself may become more robust, benefiting from other input that alters the outcome and execution of that idea. Diversity of viewpoints can allow for better execution and a greater understanding of the landscape because of the increased input that goes beyond YES.

A= NO
Q= NO   NO

R = YES YES
S = MAYBE
U = YES YES YES
T = YES MAYBE
V = YES NO
X = YES

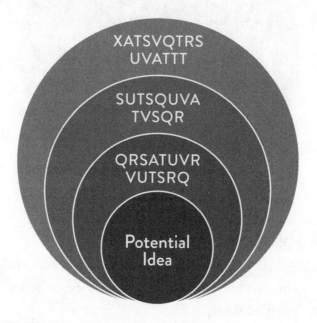

XATSVQTRS
UVATTT

SUTSQUVA
TVSQR

QRSATUVR
VUTSRQ

Potential
Idea

This is why surrounding yourself with talent, especially that which represents a diversity of viewpoints, is important for leaders. Having people around you who always say "Yes" is not to your benefit. Narcissistic leaders generally surround themselves or, I should say, insulate themselves with "Yes" people. Strong leaders surround themselves with diversity of input and viewpoints.

In their book *Begin with Trust*, authors Frances Frei and Anne Morriss use another approach to demonstrate how diversity expands the knowledge to which you have access.

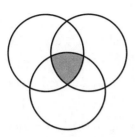

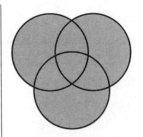

Diverse Teams	**Homogenous Teams**	**Inclusive Teams**
A diverse store of knowledge is partly shared.	A common store of knowledge is fully shared.	A diverse store of knowledge is fully shared.

Adapted from Begin with Trust [9]

What they are very careful to point out is that diversity alone is not good enough. There must be inclusivity with this diversity. So if an employee, for example, falls into the "diverse category," their presence in a decision-making room is not sufficient. One needs to feel included in order to express one's opinion and to express a diverse point of view. Diversity without inclusivity looks like the far left diagram. A team without diversity looks like the middle diagram, and a diverse and inclusive culture looks like the far right diagram. One can see that the diverse and inclusive diagram gives the greatest breadth of viewpoints and sets up a culture of more innovation. More ideas breed greater innovation.

Geography no longer dictates the search for talent. Organizations now are much more likely in their hiring to look widely and hire outside of their city, town, or even state. You could say it's another way the barriers to talent are dropping. This shift has been accelerated by the 2020 pandemic, which showed many companies the viability of remote work. I'm sure at some point many people will return to their offices, but I'm also sure that remote working will continue. Twitter CEO Jack Dorsey told employees in May 2020 that they could keep working from home indefinitely, even after COVID-19 lockdowns end. The shift to virtual everything (meetings, project management, collaboration tools) may be the biggest change we have seen to open the door to talent, wherever it resides.

Talent and diversity can be found in a global world defined not by borders but by cross-border sharing. Sharing ideas, collaborations, and initiatives to the mutual benefit of others makes a "talent strategy" much like the one that Bloomberg Philanthropies put together for college students in a collaboration with the Aspen Institute's College Excellence Program and Ithaka S+R. It is known as the American Talent Initiative (ATI). The ATI, with Dr. Dan Porterfield leading the charge, first as the president of Franklin & Marshall College and then as the president and CEO of the Aspen Institute, has set out to attract, enroll, and graduate an additional 50,000 low- and moderate-income students by 2025 at the nation's colleges and universities with the highest graduation rates. So far, ninety-seven-plus institutions have joined this initiative, including all Ivy League schools, several state flagship universities, and top liberal arts colleges.[10] This kind of initiative can be translated to all types of organizations and provides a win for the individuals and for the institutions. But I will also say that just enrolling the students into these colleges is not enough. The colleges need to have an inclusive environment where the students' diverse points of view are welcome.

Leaders can also tap into diverse thinking and points of view by looking outside their organization for sources of creativity. In this digitized and global world, collaboration need not be limited by the walls of your company: consider the value of open-source assets such as Wikipedia. Many, in fact, see the recent phenomenon of open-source technologies as the future of innovation.

Entrepreneurial activities that are fueled by diversity will inevitably be more robust as a result.

Even an individual tapping into their own "internal diversity" can enrich organizational innovation and creativity. A research team from University of Michigan and Singapore Management University found that when workers draw upon different aspects of their backgrounds, they are more creative at work. Their research focused on people who have multiple social identities, such as people who are both Asian and American, or who are both women and engineers. Through two experiments, these researchers found that people with higher levels of "identity integration" display higher levels of creativity when problems require that they draw on their different realms of knowledge. One experiment asked Asian-Americans to create new forms of Asian-American fusion cuisine, and the other asked female engineers to design a cell phone specifically for women. "Increasing creativity and innovation at work is a holy grail for organizations," said researcher Fiona Lee. "Companies that have the ability to bring together people from diverse backgrounds and draw upon all of their insights and experiences will have a distinct advantage in the global marketplace."[11]

In the next chapter, we will look very closely at ways we can mine for talent so that talent can contribute to our collective success.

As we become more diverse and differing viewpoints are expressed, we have seen that there is a tendency for some to "dig in" and wish for the "old way" of doing things. We find that as the majority becomes the minority, there can be an unwelcoming vision of the "new majority." We see that now in the United States, as the white majority becomes the minority, the struggle to hold onto power is immense. We have recently seen that by the storming of the U.S. Capitol in an attempt to change the outcome of the presidential election, as well as in the massive voter restriction laws being passed in multiple states. These represent dangers to our democracy that we must contend with. I believe that once we embrace globalization, the change in demographics, and the diversity of viewpoints, we will ultimately thrive and it may indeed offset tendencies toward division and hatred.

Land masses and boundaries separate people *and* organize them—oftentimes by nationality, race, and ethnicity—essentially keeping people of the same origins together. With the crumbling of borders comes greater diversity. In our daily lives, we regularly encounter people from a greater array of backgrounds than ever before. Pew Research Center data show: "There were a record 44.8 million immigrants living in the U.S. in 2018, making up 13.7 percent of the nation's population. This represents a more than fourfold increase since 1960, when 9.7 million immigrants lived in the U.S., accounting for 5.4 percent of the total U.S. population." [12]

Here's the paradox—as described previously, the world is globalized, and at the same time, it is polarized. While some of us embrace the world coming closer together, others resist the rapid and substantial shift to globalization.

Change, after all, can be a fearful thing. Not only that, the kind of change that comes with globalization has been politicized in recent years. In some parts of the world—even here in the United States—the diversity that results from globalization has been seen as threatening or displacing. Some people feel that the diversity that globalization presents is a threat to their lives and livelihoods. Such fears don't allow people to embrace change.

Yet without sufficient empathy, such fears are inevitable, as is the consequent polarization.

While welcoming globalization, it is important we make sure that change represents a positive influence for as many people as possible. In places in the U.S. where manufacturing or other industries have either shut down completely or been exported to other countries, there are individuals and communities who have been affected by change in the most devastating way. Some Midwest towns have generations of families who have worked in a plant or in a steel mill, and those jobs just don't exist in the same number today. People have suffered at the hands of globalization.

Sweat is a Pulitzer Prize-winning play about a group of people who work in a factory in Reading, Pennsylvania, through the decline of the early 2000s. Layoffs start chipping away at their friendships until they find themselves pitted against one another. Two women—one White, one Black—apply for the same promotion. When the Black woman gets the job, her White friend wonders if she has been favored because of her race. Tensions arising around bettering oneself with a college education, while others see it as a threat, also permeate the play. I see *Sweat* as an acutely accurate depiction of the tensions that arise when a community feels it is being left behind by change.

As leaders and people of influence, we can't just say in response, "Oh, well, the world is different now." In the same way we embrace the digital transformations that we encounter every day, we must make sure that we change education, that we change opportunity, and that we change focus. If a town loses the factory that was its main source of employment, the generational "apprenticeship model" needs to change. Perhaps families need to shed their resistance to sending their children away to college. Perhaps schools need to ensure students are taught computer skills, especially coding. In place of a notion of inherited apprenticeship, a model of more independent thinking and working may be what is needed. New models of education need to begin to populate the high school and college levels.

There is a world of difference between being a victim of change and participating in change. Only when participation occurs can those who have been negatively affected by the global changes have the means to work, to support families, and to receive the same opportunities for productive and meaningful work that globalization has brought to a newly diverse work force. Inclusivity needs to be accomplished in such a way that it assures all people that change includes them. If change does not include everyone, it will evoke fear that makes change much harder to embrace. Fear in an enemy of change.

We have seen what happens when our leaders fall short in their understanding of our newly global world. In 2020, the COVID-19 infection spread around the world. Enhanced trade and travel allowed the spread of this virus in ways that no one quite expected, especially in the United States. While earlier infections such as H1N1 and Ebola were contained to specific places in the world, the U.S. was unprepared for COVID-19.

It is clear that we can no longer operate as separate countries whose boundaries are fixed and whose food cart, clothing closet, and bank account are unaffected by what happens in what were once considered far-off lands. These lands touch our lives every single day. We can also no longer lead in a reactionary way. We have seen too much of that in the leadership of our nation, across all parties and factions. Leaders, innovators, and changemakers must look widely not only by exercising their own observational skills but by drawing around them the most diverse possible leadership group. In a word: talent.

Land masses and boundaries separate people and organize them, essentially keeping people of the same origins together. With the crumbling of borders comes greater diversity. Differing points of view and the bringing together of various skill sets and talents make a company, a school, a community, a nation more nimble, stronger, and richer.

CHAPTER 4

SEEK OUT DIVERSE TALENT

I believe that every person is born with talent.

—MAYA ANGELOU, AUTHOR

One of the greatest assets an innovator can have is the ability to nurture talent. And by that I do not mean nurturing their own talent (though that's important). I'm referring to the keen eye that some entrepreneurs have for recognizing the gifts of others and gathering skilled, accomplished people to contribute to the change the entrepreneur wants to create.

I credit Curemark's achievements in large part to our dedication to seeking excellent advisors and hiring people with many different kinds of thinking. Talent has been (and still is) very important to our company—and every company—as ideas, innovation, and execution all come from having talent within. We are a diverse group making change.

Think about the critical functions you will need to fulfill in order to succeed. Do you have the very best talent playing these roles? We must be willing to look for talent, pay for talent, and retain talent within our organizations. Talent will not show up at your doorstep. You *must* go out and find it. You must value it too; the old saying that you get what you pay for is true where talent is concerned.

If you really look for talent, you'll always get diversity. If you look for diversity, you won't always get talent. If you genuinely seek talent in all its varieties as the singular filter by which you hire employees for your business, inevitably you will accumulate a diverse team along the way. This is the fundamental difference thinking about talent that requires a new mindset in our generation.

Not long ago I was invited to a forum to discuss diversity and inclusion. The room was filled with changemakers and leaders of some of America's largest and most prestigious companies. Each of them was committed to creating positive change in their businesses and their communities, yet many of them were bemoaning the fact that their efforts to recruit diverse people kept stalling. It seemed to me—and I said as much—that even though these companies thought they were looking widely, they were really only looking inside the same box they had always looked in: the same colleges, the same geographic area, the same former employers. They needed to go out further than they ever had before to find talent and draw it in. If you believe that talent only exists in cities or is a product of graduating only from certain colleges and universities, then your search for talent to fill diverse roles will fail. Talent exists in all places and in many forms. One must go out and find it.

It's got to be done that way to get the biggest possible pool to choose from. Mine for the talent, and then hire and give them the opportunity to create. As the founder and CEO of Samasource, Leila

Janah coined the phrase: "Talent is evenly distributed, but opportunity is not." As a senior in high school, she went to Ghana on scholarship to teach English. It was during those months in Ghana that she began to understand that opportunity was not equal and that geography and distance to jobs can keep people in poverty regardless of how hard they work.[13]

Look widely and you will see talent, even where opportunity is lacking. I would go even further to say that talent creates opportunity. The two must go hand in hand. So talent, opportunity, and inclusion are key.

The same principle applies to education. If our colleges seek out young people who may not have family members or role models who attended college in the past, they will find that these first-generation college students, or "first gens," are full of talent. The pool is diverse, and it is overflowing with accomplished, motivated young people. But the onus is on colleges to look. If the colleges do not go out and find these students, they will never know there is an opportunity for them.

Colleges will need to foster and cultivate this nascent talent if that hasn't already happened at high-school level or before. But the cost is entirely worthwhile because it gives the colleges access to a much broader array of talent to educate. The follow-on is that employers have a broader array of talent to recruit, which benefits the individual organizations, the industry they occupy, their city, their state, and ultimately, the nation.

Speaking at an event at the Harvard Club in New York, Dan Porterfield—Aspen Institute president and CEO and former president of Franklin & Marshall College (F&M), where I have the honor of serving on the board of trustees—received an award on behalf of the college. He brought home the imperative to seek out and nurture the DREAMers: "Courageous undocumented teenagers and adults brought to this country as children...family-loving, law-abiding, degree-attaining, job-holding, business-creating, English-speaking, tax-paying, patriotic new Americans."[14] He acknowledged the success of F&M's talent strategy, which was being honored that evening, while at the same time affirming that it was the work of many hands—as is almost always the case with any achievement of significance. "F&M's faculty, board, funders, career center, high school partners, and, most importantly, its students and their families are the reason that we now stand as an example to the entire higher education landscape of how top colleges can open their doors to this country's full breadth of talent."

I'm a strong supporter of liberal arts education, and I believe it is important now more than ever to study widely, to have an understanding of multiple disciplines before you dive deeply into a specialization. We have no idea what skills will be needed in the workforce in twenty years' time, or even in ten years' time. What we do know is that intellectual curiosity and persistence will always be necessary for innovation. How one thinks and looks at things with a critical eye is one of the hallmarks of and the tools achieved from a liberal arts education. Those tools will remain long after a particular job or career is done or over.

It is never too early to teach those critical skills to our youth. One of the ways by which intellectual curiosity can be learned is when it is encouraged by one's peers. For example, if your child loves playing chess, he/she is likely to search out others who play chess or who will be likely to teach their friends how to play. When my nephew was in elementary school, his school offered a program where part of the class was pulled out a few times a week for a special class during which they created their own novel country. This unit ran for one semester, and by the end of fifth grade all the kids completed one semester. They had to establish a constitution, they had to run elections, and they had to choose a national song and flag. They developed a culture, maybe even a language, and all the other elements of a functional society. The whole curriculum—art, music, language arts, geography—revolved around the nation that this class was building. My nephew flourished in this class as his creativity and intellectual curiosity could be exercised to its full glory. They kept him in the program beyond his allotted one semester because his creativity helped the other kids to participate and to find their intellectual curiosity and creativity. What a great way for kids to understand the context and purpose of all the subjects they studied and to make sense of it all. It's through these kinds of creative approaches that our education system can cultivate the thinkers we need, both now and in the future.

With the right attitude and character, what you don't know you can learn. My job is to make sure my staff have the tools to do their job and the opportunity to learn what they need to learn. Hard skills can be taught, but how someone thinks is deeply important. Certain jobs require specific skills that you must know to do your job, and oftentimes you can learn them on the job. But while an employer can teach you a specific skill, they cannot teach you to think.

In my early days as a founder, there was a great deal that I didn't know. So while I had the critical skills to run a company, I did not have the familiarity with the space. I recently did an interview for *Authority Magazine*. The interview was titled "Five Things I Wish Someone Told Me Before I Became a CEO."[15] In the course of the interview I was asked, "Can you share a story about the funniest mistake you made when you were first starting?"

I told the story about how when I started Curemark over twelve years ago, I had very little experience in pharma or biotech because I did not come out of that world. I was an outsider even though I was a medical person. In the context of a conversation about the business in general, one of our lawyers asked me if I wanted an introduction to "Purdue." Because our drug is animal derived, I assumed the lawyer was offering to connect me with Perdue Farms, the chicken company.

"No, our drug is not derived from chickens," I said, a little puzzled.

She laughed. "No, I'm talking about Purdue Pharma, not Perdue Farms," she told me.

That story reflects my lack of familiarity early on with the players in the pharma space, but in no way diminishes my own talent or the talent that we have at the company. Being an outsider often can give perspective. Sometimes I would question why something was done in a particular way. So often I received the answer, "Well, that is the way it has always been done." I would perhaps suggest another way to do something and would ask if there is any reason why it couldn't be done the new way I suggested. The answer would be, "No, but it is never done that way."

We assembled a very talented team and then made sure we had access to great teachers who excelled at the regulatory aspects and who understood what our mission and our goals were. With those people on board, we could take our mission, our goals, and design a company that worked for us, that was innovative and often more efficient than doing things the old way.

Recruiting for character and talent has worked well for our company, and for our staff too. We have had the same team for more than ten years, with the exception of a couple of people who left because they moved or needed to continue their education. In a world where the average length of time a person stays with a firm is four years, that's quite a track record.[16]

Not long ago, a new board member was about to join us. I had just been in Qatar, and I met up with her at the airport in NYC so she could come into the office and meet everyone. Because it was a Friday, some of the team weren't there. We set up a Zoom call for the following week so the new board member could talk to everyone. It was deeply gratifying for me to listen to my team talk about why they're here, why the company matters to them, how much they want to bring this treatment to market, and how excited they are to have been doing this work through the years. You don't often have the opportunity to sit on the sidelines and hear those things.

The members of our team come from very different walks of life; they couldn't be more diverse, yet we share values and a vision. This work matters to us all, and we want to accomplish it ethically and correctly. The talent it takes to do that is the kind of talent I want to surround myself with.

One of the greatest assets an innovator can have is talent. By this I mean not their own talent—though they certainly need that—but the talented people they gather around them.

If you genuinely seek talent as the singular filter by which you hire employees for your business, inevitably you will accumulate a diverse team along the way. If you look for talent, you'll **always** get diversity. If you look only for diversity to check off a list, you won't always get talent.

CHAPTER 5

WELCOME DISRUPTION

Creativity is that marvelous capacity to grasp mutually distinct realities and draw a spark from their juxtaposition.

—MAX ERNST, GERMAN PAINTER AND SCULPTOR

Space is the final frontier, or so they say. This has been true for a very long time. For as long as we have recorded history, the great thinkers, scientists, mathematicians, and philosophers have been examining space. Not "outer space," but a more all-encompassing concept, classically defined as "the area in which everything exists."

Here are some of the greatest "space explorers" our world has ever seen:

Aristotle (384–322 BC) studied the potentiality of objects both in motion and rest. He also described a geometric model for our solar system where the sun, moon, stars, and planets revolved around Earth, each in its own space.

Isaac Newton (1643–1727) was responsible for formulating the laws of motion and the foundation of our understanding of gravity.

Gottfried Liebniz (1646–1716) examined kinetic and potential energy. He developed the notion of integral calculus and the concept of topology as the distance between two or more points.

Carl Friedrich Gauss (1777–1855) calculated the appearance of the dwarf planet Ceres in the sky using comprehensive approximation methods that he developed specially for that purpose. This work led Gauss to develop a theory of the motion of planetoids disturbed by large planets.

Albert Einstein (1879–1955) devised his theory of relativity, which recognized that the placement of two objects and the space between them is key.

Max Ernst (1891–1976) was a pioneer of the Dada movement and surrealism. His dreamlike paintings used collage techniques to combine and juxtapose seemingly unrelated elements, giving them a new significance.

We can see that the study of two objects in relation to each other and the space between those objects has historically been very important to leading scientists, artists, mathematicians, and others who demonstrate a unique level of curiosity about the world around them. Space matters, and not just for philosophers and mathematicians. Paying attention to the space between objects and the space around an object—and consequently around us and all we do—is important for us innovators too.

Let me explain that idea a little more. By definition, space is the area in which everything exists. In that "space" can exist a single object with only space around it. In contrast to the juxtaposition of one or more objects to another or others, I call the singular object with space around it "**Just-A-Position**." Studying and contrasting the **Juxtaposition** of two objects, particles, or other discreet masses with "space" between them tells us much more. Describing something as it is—just a position—gives limited information relative to describing two objects and their relation-ship to each other—juxtaposition.

In the following table, you will see a list of things that are Just-A-Position contrasted with those that are in Juxtaposition.

Just-A-Position	Juxtaposition
One thing in space	More than one thing
Fixed	Fluid
Singularity	Variety
No combinations	Limitless combinations
Stagnation	Growth
Non-idea generating	Idea generating
Hinders connection	Promotes connection

We see that **Just-A-Position** is really a moment in time, a place to have perspective but not specifics, whereas **Juxtaposition** has meaning with respect to the space between two objects. Now that we have expanded the relationship of space and objects beyond the basic science, let's take it another step. We often describe the "status quo" as a continuous line, the same thing repeated over again to make an unbroken whole. Said another way, the status quo is thought to be "what has always been," what comes from many moments of Just-A-Position in a continuous broken line.

I have long held the opinion that while most people look at the status quo as a continuous line, I believe that it is not a continuous line, but rather, one that has many breaks in it—multiple spaces.

I believe that innovation and change come out of the "seams" (spaces) in the status quo, and what is on either side of the seam is key to having that view or sense of space between the beginning and end of that line. Within these breaks or seams in the status quo comes a new energy, and with that energy comes change and innovation.

Innovation, therefore, is not truly *de novo*, but an outgrowth of what we already experience and what has always been.

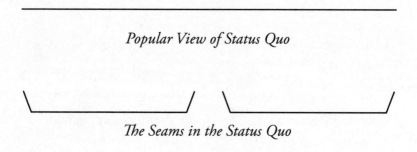

Popular View of Status Quo

The Seams in the Status Quo

One of the most powerful seams—or spaces—on Earth is the San Andreas Fault. Running along the coast of California, it has long been recognized as the source of what could be a catastrophic earthquake in San Francisco or Los Angeles—or for that matter, anywhere along its path. While the fault represents a break in the earth's crust, we understand that the space between the two earth plates can generate powerful energy from within. When those plates move, shear, or buckle against one another, they can cause an earthquake where the energy in the seams is released. Such an earthquake can generate powerful destructive forces that can alter the landscape for eons. From within that space, then, comes change.

San Andreas Fault

What occupies the seams, or spaces, matters. Take a pile of bricks. They could represent a major impediment for someone or something trying to get beyond the pile. You could call them an obstacle to passage. If you start your car, hit the accelerator, and drive it straight at the pile, you will displace some bricks. Your car will probably get dented and scratched in the process, but it's likely some bricks will fall over, and the pile will move slightly. There is give between the bricks, but they are only moving relative to the force of the car, their own weight, and the friction that is created between the bricks.

@divide_by_zero

If you then take that same pile of bricks and put cement between the individual bricks, the pile of bricks becomes a wall.

@jonatanlindemann

It is the substance that has been placed in the space between the bricks that creates a wall, with greater tensile strength than that of the bricks just stacked one on another. This time, if you drive your car into the wall, it is likely to cause much more damage to your vehicle and will not displace the bricks very much, if at all.

Two very different outcomes resulting from an interaction between two objects. The wall is nothing more than the bricks with something in the space between them, and that is sufficient to give the bricks different meaning and purpose.

Space matters!

The COVID-19 pandemic has highlighted the importance of "space." So no discussion of space would be complete without a mention of the social and physical distancing that we experienced during the pandemic, as well as a century earlier during the 1918 influenza pandemic. This distancing became a hallmark of the pandemic, and what has emerged from this distance has changed our perspective on many things and has resulted in innovation, ranging from food services to medical delivery.

One way in which the spread of a virus is reduced is to maintain a physical distance from others. In the vernacular we call it "social distancing," but it is actually physical distance that we put between ourselves and others. As humans we struggle with physical distancing because it impairs one of the ways through which we communicate with others. We are, after all, fundamentally social beings.

The difficulty people have with social distancing, I believe, has to do with the fact that the recommended distance of six feet interferes with some the very basic tools that we as humans use to navigate our world. Besides the most obvious inability to use our sense of touch at that distance, six feet distance puts us at the very outer limits of our ability to hear another human speak. The male voice at a normal level can be heard at a distance of 6 to 6.5 feet. That puts a woman's voice at slightly under that distance. If we can't hear one another, it robs us of the ability to express ourselves to other humans and for them to properly respond.

I'm going to add to this our ability to smell. Our sense of smell plays a threefold role. First, our physical attraction to others relies, in part, on smell. The role of pheromones and other hormones have long been studied; researchers go so far as to say that "our body odour, produced by the genes which make up our immune system, can help us subconsciously choose our partners." [17] Humans also use smell to alert us to dangers such as fire or rotten food. And perhaps more than any other sense, smell is closely linked to memory and emotion. People who lose their sense of smell report feeling isolated and cut off. It is interesting to note that the SARS-CoV-2 virus that produces the COVID-19 infection alters the sense of taste and smell in many who contract the virus. It is almost as if this virus tries to drive us closer to people to increase infection rates through the loss of taste and smell. We also must add here there is a reduction of the sense of smell through the use of a mask.

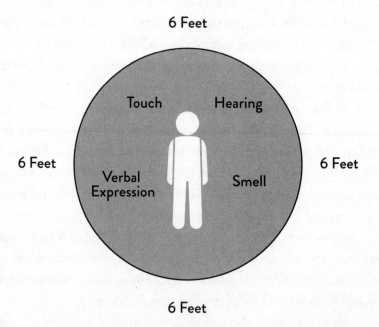

So within six feet of distance lies a space where we can most effectively and fully use our senses of hearing, touch, and smell, along with the ability to express ourselves verbally and to receive that communication. Outside of that six feet, we begin to lose the sound of voices, the smell of others, and the ability to touch someone.

These senses and levels of expression are all needed for us to navigate our world. They give us a level of social proprioception that I think everyone is longing for during the pandemic.

Right now, I believe we are in a "seam time" in the status quo. The COVID-19 pandemic caused the seams in the status quo to appear enlarged in a way that the entire world can see many of them. The year 2020 was hard and the future is going to be hard too.

Not only did the seams in the status quo become more visible, the pandemic created an entirely new status quo in many areas: where we work, where and what we eat, how we learn and go to school, and mostly with whom we interact on a daily basis. Even how we interact with one another has changed and become a "new normal." All of a sudden, people needed ways to get their food delivered, ways to have meetings from their home, ways to exercise without going to the gym, and ways to learn without being in a classroom.

Let's take telemedicine, which owes its development in part to space explorers of a different kind—the ones we met at the start of this chapter. One of the first applications of telemedicine was in the late 1960s when NASA needed to monitor the physical condition of its astronauts in zero gravity.[18] Telemedicine has been around for many, many years, but it was taking a long time to be widely accepted. Existing medical mores and traditions in medicine have allowed the field to drag its feet with respect to remote health monitoring. It was generally perceived as a relief measure for developing nations where there were few physicians and populations were scattered across remote villages, or as a way for doctors to read scans in a remote hospital that only had a part-time radiologist or none at all. The immediacy of remote care that has presented itself during the pandemic has pushed the acceptance of telemedicine ahead twenty years. In 2020, there was no other viable choice: either you visited your doctor remotely or you went without care. This presented an underutilization of well-care and basic symptom care. So many individuals missed their regular check-ups. The stress of the pandemic also created a tremendous uptick in the use of mental health visits, and I suspect this higher volume will continue post-pandemic.

Video conferencing is another example. The modality already existed, and it was used widely by businesses and some individuals. But in 2020, when face-to-face interaction became increasingly difficult due to COVID-19, video conferencing, and more specifically Zoom (which had more recently rolled out its platform) became the best way to have a meeting. In just one month, video conferencing apps saw a record 62 million downloads.[19] As businesses switched to remote working to limit the spread of COVID-19, platforms such as Google Hangouts, Microsoft Teams, Cisco Webex, and Zoom became essential working tools. At the time we may have thought these were stopgap measures, but "Zoom" has become a generic term—like Kleenex or Uber—and is a popular option for everything from family reunions and industry conferences to BFF catch-ups and first dates.

Our Gen Z children were already digital natives long before the pandemic struck. Seemingly arriving in the world with an iPad and/or phone already firmly gripped in their hand, today's children are much more at home with technology than their parents. When children are growing up there are guidelines for developmental milestones that have been around for a long time. I believe that at some point they are likely to add "swiping" as a pediatric developmental milestone; many children learn to swipe through their parents' phone quite early in their lives as their parents hand the phone to their child to look at pictures . . . through which they need to "swipe." All kidding aside, there is likely to be a recognized skill of "swiping" in the future.

Prior to 2020, there had been many attempts to unseat the status quo in many arenas. In education, the entire system has been resistant to change. Then in 2020, the education system had to follow a path that had been opened up when there was little choice but to use distance and online learning. There needed to be a pivot to remote learning on a massive scale due to the COVID-19 pandemic. For many educators, it has been quite the tremor. Some liberal arts colleges were adamantly against the notion of online classes. The premise of the liberal arts is to teach an individual how to think, how to integrate multiple disciplines, and how one discipline influences another. This is often done in a very experiential way that needs face-to-face contact with instructors and peers. Come 2020, colleges had to pivot and change fast to a hybrid or fully online class structure. The new model was embraced well and uncovered some new techniques and values in an online environment that many did not anticipate nor would have uncovered had they not been forced to pivot.

Now think again about a child with Autism. Many of them need a one-on-one focused learning environment. The pandemic hits and they are forced to be at home and online. For some it is a blessing as they learn best from a computer screen and no longer have to deal with peers and the busy environment of their classroom. For others the one-on-one and ancillary services that are missing have been coupled with a family structure that does not allow concerted focused efforts on their learning—as, perhaps, there are two or three other siblings also learning at home. The changes in learning mandated by the pandemic created both hardships and opportunities.

I don't see this pivot as a temporary fix. I have always seen education as a hybrid of classic education: book and classroom learning as well as experiential learning. I see the future of education as an immersive experience. Both short-term and even longer-term, I would love to see college students coming on campus in one- or two-week increments to have 24/7 immersive time with a small group of their peers and their professor. This way they would have a truly memorable, intense experience, followed by independent time to assimilate the hands-on and face-to-face learning and/or to implement what they learned in the real world. I attended F&M College, which prides itself on excellence in a liberal arts education through immersive and experiential learning. Forty years later, I can still recall most of those experiential learning opportunities I had as a student. They taught me important things that I continue to use in my work today.

I recently had the opportunity to communicate my thanks to one of my professors Dr. Nancy McDowell, who forty-five years ago took me to meet Dr. Margaret Mead. Having spent a good deal of the semester studying the Mudugumor people, a tribe in Papua, New Guinea, with Dr. McDowell, I can remember that day we met Dr. Mead as if it were yesterday. Dr. Mead had also studied the Mudugumors many years before Professor McDowell. It was such an honor to make the short trip with Dr. McDowell to Maryland with a few other students to meet Dr. Mead and to see her give what was likely one of her last public talks, as she died of pancreatic cancer two years later. As I said, Dr. McDowell had studied the Mundugumors of Papua, New Guinea, just as Dr. Mead had before her. Dr. Mead entrusted many of her field notes from her own study of the Mundugumors to Dr. McDowell. The link of the classroom with the immersive experience was memorable, and it was such a terrific teaching tool. Dr. McDowell made specific references throughout the semester to their differing views of the people they'd both studied, and how perspective and observation differ depending upon who makes those observations—their past, their education, and who influenced them. This lesson was quite a valuable one, and to see their differing styles and approaches on display was a fabulous lesson.

I've been told that my in-and-out residence model of learning doesn't fit the current financial model that most, if not all, residential colleges are based upon, but in my view, it would be a powerful way for students to learn. Students could be working in the field or on projects when they're not in a classroom. It is more of a postgraduate model, the kind of model I've pursued myself in my summer learning experiences, so it is not something people think about applying to undergraduates or even high school students.

Nothing is beyond innovating. Even the most traditional products and pastimes can benefit from change. Take baseball, a truly slow-changing sport that cherishes its heritage. In recent decades, the biggest change was the rush to analytics, moving from a game that operated on pure gut feel to one driven by the numbers. Then 2020 came around, and teams had to postpone games, make them up later, and play a compressed schedule because of the pandemic. One solution was to play doubleheaders (two games on one day) of a shortened duration (seven innings each). The standard length of baseball games has been nine innings—even before the professional league began in 1869. But maybe there's a place for shorter games; it might be a way to bring in families and younger fans who don't want to sit through a game that runs for three hours or more. To the diehards, a seven-innings game is blasphemy. But in this "seam time" in the break in the status quo, we can see the need for change more clearly. For one, it is likely that fewer players could be injured or suffer fatigue from playing three nine-inning games in a two-day period.

Sometimes as a society, we have change forced upon us. It may be forced by an unanticipated political shift or a cataclysmic event such as a pandemic or war.

The gaps in the status quo won't go away. The status quo won't snap back like an elastic band to the same length it was before. Instead, the seams will be filled with innovation, and they will become part of a new form of status quo.

> **Innovation and change come out of the seams (spaces) in the status quo. Within these breaks or seams in the status quo comes a new energy, and with that energy comes change and innovation.**

SECTION 2

IMPEDIMENTS TO CHANGE

HOW TO OVERCOME
EXTERNAL OBSTACLES
AND INTERNAL BARRIERS
(BOTH REAL AND PERCEIVED)

CHAPTER 6

FILTER THE NOISE

*Because one believes in oneself, one doesn't try to
convince others. Because one is content with oneself,
one doesn't need others' approval. Because one accepts
oneself, the whole world accepts him or her.*

—Lao Tzu, Ancient Chinese Philosopher

When you are responsible for something—whether it's coaching a basketball team, running a company, or even parenting a newborn baby—it seems like everyone has an opinion to offer. Every acquaintance, neighbor, and random stranger wants to give their two cents. Apparently, they feel it's their job to push or pull you in a direction of their choosing. Suddenly you're deafened by all the voices.

Maybe humans are hardwired to be helpful—that's a charitable way of seeing it. You could also say that we're hardwired to super-impose our thoughts, beliefs, and ideas on others.

When you are highly visible in the world, it will be human nature for others to suggest, cajole, offer, insinuate, or just plain tell you what to do. It happens all the time. Take a pregnant woman for example. Complete strangers think it is perfectly okay for them to rub her baby bump, offer their guesses at the sex of the baby (even if she doesn't know or care to share), and then offer parenting advice, especially if it is a first child. Often, they take time to reminisce about their own pregnancies or their own children. Politicians, athletes, and coaches are public figures who often receive mounds of unsolicited advice. Every day, newspapers, television news, and social media are filled with often uninformed people with the best of intentions who just want to "help out" with a few suggestions.

"Why didn't the manager pull that pitcher before he lost control of his pitches and lost us the game?"

"Why does our congressional representative feel she has to vote that way? We elected her; why is she voting that way?"

"She's clearly lost a step on the court—can't she see it's time to retire? And she needs to shorten that backswing."

The voices from the self-appointed experts on the sidelines can be *loud*.

As an entrepreneur or leader, many people will offer you advice too. They will hold out to you the opportunity to benefit from their wisdom—to lead you out of trouble, or on the next step in your venture, or whatever they discern as your most pressing need. But this is not an empathic approach that we talk about earlier in this book. Mostly they are trying to convey their own experience or thoughts, or how they would do something. There is something deep inside us that compels us to make another human think, believe, or do as we do all in the name of "helping." It affirms us;

it makes us feel good. While some of their advice may be useful, it takes time and much filtering to know what is and isn't important.

I call all of it *noise*. While professional athletes can choose to stop reading the newspapers or watching the TV broadcasts, it can be harder for entrepreneurs to switch off the soundtrack of peers, investors, friends, or family members who feel it is their duty to insert themselves into the conversation they imagine we are having in our heads. Sometimes it is hard to separate from these conversations because the lines and boundaries are blurred. For example, you may not need or want an uninformed position, or maybe you needed that less-informed opinion earlier in your journey but now it is not helpful because you are further along in your journey. Their perspective is no longer helpful.

All of this noise can be a distraction and a hindrance if we allow it to predominate in our lives. Yet at the same time, cutting yourself off from it entirely does a disservice to you and to your venture. There is a balance to be struck between the kind of noise that is helpful and that which is not, between the amount of noise that is beneficial and the amount that gets in the way.

Imagine that you are a golfer competing in the U.S. Open. Standing out there on the links at Pebble Beach, you must consider many things before taking a swing:

- Distance to the hole
- Lie and type of grass or sand
- Grass height
- Wind speed
- Green elevation
- Slope
- Number and nature of obstacles
- Overall weather conditions
- Your ability to hit for distance
- Your ability to use a specific wood or iron club

• The loft of your club

That's not an exhaustive list by any means, and yet all this data must be synthesized. Your brain must process a huge aggregate of information, and then put all that input into your next swing.

SYNTHESIS OF ALL INFORMATION => SWING

The same is true of the way you process information as a founder, innovator, or changemaker. Consider it carefully, understand the biases and influences that are relevant, tap into your own internal and external data, and then aggregate it all to determine what your next move is going to look like.

You cannot make your best shot if you are second-guessing yourself, delaying a decision, allowing yourself to be overwhelmed with the pundits' advice, or letting one thought override all others. Once you acquire the relevant information, you must set out a real plan and then follow it. Good golfers do this—and great golfers do it best of all.

All of us are exposed to so much more information nowadays than when I grew up. Once, news would have passed through filters; imagine it as being like different sizes of mesh sorting data. If you read a medical article in *Good Housekeeping*, say, you could ascribe a certain value to it. It would be accessible to you, perhaps something you read while waiting in the dentist office. In academia it would be considered a secondary or tertiary source article. An article on the same topic in *The New England Journal of Medicine* would have a different value and would be considered a primary source article as generally it would be based upon data gathered by the authors. When I went to college, if you wanted to look up a specific topic in medicine located in a medical journal, you had to go to the library and access huge bound volumes called *Indicus Medicus* (IM) that listed all of the medical journals. In the IM you would be led to the primary source articles on specific topics. Then you had to go to find that journal in the "stacks." Further, if you were looking for a topic with current literature, you had to wait for the monthly supplements to arrive in the library so that you could look up the topics.

Back then, the journals had a specific look and feel to them: solid, well-produced, skillfully edited, and typeset unlike other publications. You could tell by the way each journal or book was presented that it was a professional publication. You can't do that anymore. It's certainly wonderful that you can access *The New England Journal of Medicine* online, but you may equally stumble across some entirely fabricated article or publication that looks equally authoritative to the untrained eye. Now everything is equally accessible to us all. This is certainly a great leveler. So while access to information has increased, which is good, the quality of that information is often hard to discern. At times it feels as if we are being assaulted by a high-pressure hose on full bore—there is no filter, no barrier, to soften the deluge of information.

It is more important than ever to do your own filtering. Apply your own mesh by considering which sources you can trust. Volume is no guide; unreliable voices can be just as loud as the trustworthy ones—or even louder. Facebook, Twitter, and other sources of information have very poor filters.

Tuning out the noise is easier if you have brought good advisers to your venture. These are people you can listen to. A pro golfer may not listen to the 25,000 pundits tweeting at them during a tournament, but they will listen to their caddy. They will filter and aggregate, taking the important considerations into account.

But in the end, it is the golfer who must swing that club, not any trusted adviser, caddie, or self-appointed expert.

If you are becoming distracted by the noise, apply your own filters to tune it out. Learn how to aggregate the right kinds of information to make a plan. Then, like a champion golfer, you can make that perfect swing, the one that enables you to win the tournament.

In business I find that there's an assumption that when someone talks a big game, it must be real. Bravado drowns out all the evidence to the contrary—because very often, the people doing the most talking are not always getting things done.

A friend of mine took over a sizeable company a few years back, and I acted as an adviser to him as he set a new direction for the company. The middle and upper management was full of "noisemakers"—that's the best term I can think of for these people, who were just full of themselves but didn't get anything significant done. They kept the status quo as steady as it could be. Moreover, this same group of people was often the most unyielding to change and often obstructionist to change that could displace them or change the nature of the organization. They often blocked promotions that were not in their best interest and prevented others from making progress too. Mostly they talked incessantly about their accomplishments and made it appear that they were the machine behind the organization. These "noisemakers" have a tendency to permeate organizations, burrow in, and keep all others out. It's like a self-perpetuating ecosystem. So while these noisemakers may talk about how open and progressive they are, in reality their presence in a company make it far less progressive and open to diversity, inclusivity, and change.

I told my friend he had to get rid of some of these people, but he was initially conflicted. "Who would hire them if I let them go?" he asked me. "They are older, very highly paid, and they live in an old paradigm."

"So do you keep them and handicap your organization further, and acquiesce to a group of individuals who live above their ability, their vision, and their pay grade?" I responded.

Ultimately my friend moved many of these executives out of the organization.

Clearly these ensconced individuals live not in a place of self-belief, but in another paradigm entirely. You will find them in some cases in leadership roles but *not* acting as leaders. Instead, they exhibit the kind of defensive, dug-in style they need to maintain their positions and their egos.

I've often wondered why certain people feel they have to bluster their way through. At one time I thought, well, they just like to hear themselves speak. They must love the sound of their own voices. But I have come to another conclusion. I believe that they use their voices much like echolocation. Bats, dolphins, and other animals use this mechanism to make sense of their environment. The animal makes a sound and then listens for the echoes from the sound waves bouncing off their surroundings. The interpretation of the waves, the timing, and the timbre of the sound that comes back to them allow them to gather enormous amounts of information. This way, they can avoid obstacles, find prey, and avoid predators. When people make a lot of noise, the responses they get back tell them where everybody sits: is *this* colleague an obstacle to my plan? Is *that* manager my ally or my enemy? Taking the temperature of those around them is a hallmark of these noisemakers.

The presence of self-belief allows us to tune out the noise. I define self-belief as the understanding that you have the ability, understanding, and capacity to perform a particular task and the confidence to do it. Just knowing that you have those abilities is not enough to accomplish a task. Believing you have the ability and the confidence to carry it out is what I am speaking to. If you have self-belief, there's no need for all the noise. True confidence and authority tend to be on the quiet side.

It seems to me that there is an inverse relationship between the amount of noise a person makes about their ideas and achievements and the extent to which they truly believe in themselves. Self-belief begins with action, not talk.

I am not talking about ego here, and I am not talking about bullying your way through a situation. I am talking about having a firm belief in *you*. This kind of belief doesn't need hype. This kind of belief understands the need for self-care as a part of your repertoire, and that taking care of your own body, mind, and soul is paramount in a fully functioning productive adult. When you are engaged in these types of actions, there is little need to talk about self, as the feedback comes from within, and is not external.

So many of us derive our self-worth from the people around us. We lean on others' assessments of our value, our efforts, our potential. You could have a thousand people cheering you on, but no number of other people believing in you can compensate for a lack of belief in yourself.

Self-belief is the foundation of who we are, determining where we start and where we end in everything we do. This self-belief allows us to be criticized, it allows us to move forward, it allows us to get up when we trip. Most of all, it allows us to be magnanimous, gracious, and empathetic to others.

Of all the qualities that you will need as an innovator or change-maker, none is as essential as self-belief. You can believe in your product, you can believe in your team, you can believe in the path you have chosen to move forward, and you can even believe that others believe in you. But if you don't believe in yourself, none of this means very much at all.

Here are three valuable things I have learned about self-belief:

1. Self-belief allows you to learn from your mistakes and to grow.
2. Self-belief can see you through all the ups and downs of your entrepreneurial journey.
3. Self-belief allows us to be fully empathetic.

Let's break those thoughts down in more detail.

When you cultivate self-belief, mistakes become learning opportunities. A mistake does not mean that you are incompetent, reckless, or unable to do your job—it simply means that you made "not the best choice." Nothing more. When you believe in yourself, mistakes become the teacher.

Trial-and-error learning is woven into entrepreneurship because you are trying to do something that is novel. Just as we saw in chapter 1 when looking at the d.school at Stanford, when you do something novel, it's like any kind of experimentation: you will have a process of trial-and-error, and it is through that process that you will refine your concept. Mistakes are simply part of the learning.

At Stanford's d.school they talk a lot about working through different iterations of a product or service so that you come out in the end with the right one. If you step into that process feeling fearful of making a mistake or not trusting yourself to find the best outcome, you are presetting the program to "failure mode." In the next chapter we'll take a look at the differences between mistakes and failures. For now, think of it as taking the emotional heat out of mistakes, seeing them as part of a scientific process of experimentation.

What we learn through this process helps us to grow. This growth is a part of the fabric.

Self-belief guards against burnout. When you believe in yourself, you will have the stamina to withstand the bumps and bruises that will inevitably come your way in the entrepreneurial journey, and you will be able to keep going. Without self-belief, each bump will become encased in a coating of self-doubt, making the bumps become bigger than they truly are. The bumps then can become obstacles.

Each time we experience a down moment or we hit issues in our lives as an entrepreneur, a parent, or whatever role, we have the ability to bounce back, though the ability to change the "down" to an "up" requires a period of time. In science it is often called a refractory period, a period where things return to another state. Having a strong belief in oneself allows this time to pass as we regain strength and refuse to dwell on the down.

Self-belief gives us resilience and strength.

Self-belief enables empathy. To be fully empathetic, we must be able to go beyond ourselves, our self-obsession, and our self-interest to place ourselves in someone else's shoes. In our chapter on empathy, we will see how important it is to be empathetic to solve problems. It all starts with self-belief, which empowers others and gives you a sure footing to give to others and to share yourself.

My view is that self-belief comes out of a little bit of nature and a little bit of nurture. In fact, I'd say it's a little bit of nature and a *lot* of nurture. When I was growing up, the message my parents consistently delivered to my brother and me was that we could be anything we wanted to be—and if they could help us, they would. At the EY Strategic Growth Forum in 2017, I had the privilege of hearing sporting legends Shaquille O'Neal and Billie Jean King speak in separate sessions. While they are two very different types of elite athletes, one thing they said about their upbringing was remarkably similar. After a match or a game their parents never asked them whether they won or lost. They always asked them *how they played.* Both of these outstanding athletes had parents who were concerned for their child, not their child's win/loss performance. Both sets of parents understood that how their child played and the child's own assessment of their performance were most important. Not only does that set the scene for strong internal motivation, but it also lays the groundwork for a child to believe in themselves.

This is how you nurture internal motivation: by encouraging your children, your team members, and your peers to do the very best they are capable of. Otherwise, we will always be looking for the win, the win, the win.

Not all of us have the benefit of such remarkable parents with this attitude, and not everyone has parents or even a parent who has the time to help their child achieve their goals. Many parents work multiple jobs and do everything they can to provide for their children. A generational cycle of poverty, abuse, neglect, or inattention is one of the hardest things to escape. It is not impossible, however. A mentor can make all the difference to a young person who is not brought up to believe in themselves; offering a positive influence can help them immensely.

I mentioned earlier a young player for the Yankees who is a personal favorite of mine. When he first joined the team, Clint Frazier was young and some would say brash. His favorite number is seven, but the best Yankees player ever (Mickey Mantle) wore that number. Wishing he could wear #7, Clint settled on #77.

Clint is amazingly talented. He struggled while he shuttled between the AAA minor club and the Major Leagues. One day I had the opportunity to have a conversation with him when I was asked by some of the Yankees brass to share my own journey and how one perseveres to a goal. Toward the end of our discussion I said, "Just remember you are a unique talent; just let your bat and your glove do your talking. Keep your head down and let that amazing talent take over." Clint went back down the minors, worked very hard on perfecting his skills, and when he finally came up to the Major League club at the end of last season, his bat and his glove did all the talking. Whatever self-doubt he had, whatever he struggled with internally, seemed to vanish and he excelled. He excelled so much so that he was one of three finalists nominated for a Gold Glove, which is given to the best defensive player at each position in each league.

Now Clint has begun to believe in himself in amazing ways. In the midst of the pandemic in 2020, this young man stood out from the other players because he wore a mask for the entire game. Whether he was on the bench, out on the field, or up to bat, the mask was on.

"Why are you wearing your mask all the time?" a reporter asked him.

"Look, we are in a pandemic, and it protects me, but it mostly protects you," he replied. In that response this young man showed a tremendous amount of empathetic maturity and responsible behavior. He had gotten himself to a place where he was able to speak to his beliefs without fear.

No matter whether you're a pro athlete, a rising entrepreneur, a founder, or an agent of change, it is as Lao Tzu says. Believe in yourself and you don't need to convince others or seek their approval. When you accept yourself, the whole world will accept you too.

Having self-belief allows you to tune out the noise, learn from your mistakes, and make leadership decisions that are empathetic, effective, future-focused, and wise.

CHAPTER 7

LOGIC AND DATA STILL PREVAIL

You can't cross the sea merely by standing and staring at the water.

—RABINDRANATH TAGORE, BENGALI POLYMATH

In business and in life, logic matters a great deal. Hans Halvorson, in his book *How Logic Works*, lays out why logic is important in our lives.[20] He depicts it as a skill we should all have in order to operate effectively, make and understand arguments, and communicate what we are thinking. He offers three reasons we should understand and use logic:

1. It will help you get what you want by communicating what you need.
2. Many of the new jobs in our society require logic skills.

3. Regardless of one's religious beliefs or political bent, logic will help us to be sure that our views align with reality.

Bad, illogical, or willful arguments are made every day in every walk of life. If you are a parent, you will hear some of the most illogical arguments of all time from your children. While a child can be compelling with their emotion and desire for a specific outcome, their arguments are often so illogical that it undermines their argument. Wanting something doesn't make it so.

In 2020 some of our elected officials pushed to change the outcome of our presidential election, defying the Constitution and the very oath they took to uphold. While the "changers" claimed election fraud, in almost sixty lawsuits no one could produce any evidence. When they yelled fraud on the courtroom steps, when they entered the courtroom and addressed a judge, they could come up with no evidence of fraud.

Even with that failure, there were dozens of U.S. senators and congresspersons echoing the fraud claim, wanting to overturn the outcome of the presidential election so that "the will of the people is actually carried out," or so they claimed. While the election ballot counting had been done multiple times in multiple arenas and was certified by all fifty states, these senators and congresspersons—some of whom were elected on those same ballots—continued to make an argument that the outcome of the presidential election was not valid. The will of the people was the outcome of the election, not what they wanted.

Here we have a situation where there was no logic applied, the arguments were willful and inaccurate, and yet the "changers" continued to push them as though they were truthful. Because the arguments were so illogical, understanding them was difficult and the *only* way to deal with them was to remain grounded in logical reasoning and the truth. Repeating untruths does not make them truthful. Espousing a lack of reality does not make it so. The courts have started to push back against these lawyers.

In his three reasons for logic, Halvorson makes it clear that without logic we can end up in a place where reality is lacking. Ultimately, with enough illogical thinking, we find ourselves living outside reality entirely.

In business we apply reasoning in so many ways: to figure out the cause of a glitch in our manufacturing process, to determine the size of the market for our service, or to understand the best way for our company to respond to an economic downturn.

There is more than one kind of reasoning to choose from, however. People tend to apply just one kind when they would gain a more complete understanding by applying two forms of reasoning—or more.

If you've ever studied science, law, or even criminology, you've most likely heard about the concepts of deductive and inductive reasoning. Both are effective tools for navigating real-life problems, but they approach the same question from opposite directions.

Deductive reasoning, or deduction, starts with a general statement, theory, or hypothesis, brings in observation, and examines the possibilities to reach a specific, logical conclusion.

In deductive reasoning, everything depends upon the original general statement, hypothesis, or theory being correct. If it is, we can likely predict what the observations should be. If the original theory or statement is incorrect, we will not see the expected observations, nor will our conclusion be correct.

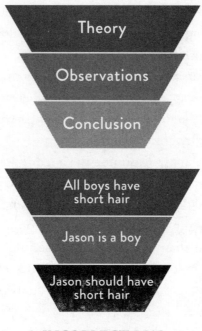

INCORRECT BIAS

When we see that Jason actually has long hair, it means that our original theory was incorrect. The incorrect original theory was clearly and easily disproved.

CORRECT BIAS

In this scenario, our theory turns out to be correct as all newborns do grow.

One of the times when we most recently saw that deductive reasoning did not result in a good outcome is what turned out to be an overuse of ventilators to treat COVID-19 infections. Conventional medicine told us that at a certain time in an individual's illness it was time to use a ventilator. This was based on certain tests and observations made in a specific presenting case. Ventilators were often applied based upon this theory and these observations, but in certain cases of COVID-19 we found out that using ventilators may worsen the condition.

Inductive reasoning is essentially the opposite of deductive reasoning. While deductive reasoning starts with a premise or a theory, inductive reasoning starts with specific observations from which we make broad generalizations or construct a theory. Usually referred to as inferences, the conclusions reached from inductive reasoning rely on discrete observations.

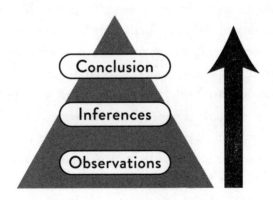

While deductive reasoning starts from the general and drills down to the more specific, and inductive reasoning starts with individual observations and makes generalizations from those observations, both of these suffer from potential biases. Inductive reason suffers from potential bias because the observational sample could be too small or unrepresentative of the larger population. Deductive reasoning suffers from the expectation that if a premise is true, then the consequence is also true. The best example of this is, in David Hitchcock's words: "If it's a duck, it quacks; and it quacks, so it must be a duck." (Or maybe it's a decoy.[21])

One of the most important tenets of research is that it *must* be generalizable to a larger population. A common error in research, especially in the collection of data, is the use of a biased or unrepresentative sample. For example, many studies in psychology use undergraduate psychology students as their subjects, but these students may not be representative of the "universe" to which the studies' authors wish to generalize their results. This kind of biased sampling is a prevalent flaw in public opinion polling.

Also, this kind of bias is often seen in clinical trials with respect to minority participation. In the COVID-19 vaccine trials one of the companies boasted that they conducted 21 percent of the trial on individuals over sixty-five years of age. When the ages were broken down, only approximately 4 percent was tested on individuals over seventy-five years of age. But why was that if the very first group of people to be vaccinated under the emergency authorization approval included those over seventy-five? Well, traditionally the elderly do not mount the same immune response to vaccinations, such the flu vaccine, as younger people do. It is why the flu vaccine is available in two strengths and those over sixty-five should get the stronger one. That way, when the vaccine manufacturer reports the efficacy results from the clinical trials and how much immune response there is, it will not be reduced due to the lack of immune response by older subjects.

Another area of bias is with hypertension, where instead of people of specific ages being overtly excluded, people of color are.

In theory, all people are welcome to participate as long as you are within the age range required. However, subjects with diabetes and/or heart disease are often excluded. The common reasoning is that those with hypertension and co-occurring diabetes or heart disease could confound the results and "muffle" the "data signal." There are large numbers of individuals with hypertension and these co-occurring conditions among Black men and women and people of color. These three often occur together. It is true, however, once a drug is approved, it will be used by people of color who suffer from these co-occurring conditions even if it has not been tested on them.

Both inductive and deductive reasoning require the right amount of information in order to bring us to reasonable conclusions. If we have seen ten brown ducks in our local pond, we could use induction to conclude that all the ducks in this particular pond are brown. But we need more evidence to support our claim; there could be five white ducks nesting just out of sight in the next inlet. So if we waited longer and found or saw the white ducks, our conclusion would be different. Deduction, on the other hand, could lead us to say, "A cat has four paws. My pet has four paws. Therefore, my pet is a cat." In this case, the initial premise is too specific. There are many animals with four paws, so your pet could be anything from a Corgi to a crested gecko—not necessarily a cat at all.

Inductive reasoning is very prone to error, even more so than deductive reasoning. Yet we tend to default to the inductive approach—I suspect in part because it produces hard data. You must acquire more pieces of information, which all come at a price and therefore one must pay for that data. The inductive process is therefore easier to commercialize. Our education system is also geared toward inductive reasoning, and yet a deductive system founded on good information and well-tested contains fewer errors. The education model has been based upon small facts that are aggregated into a conclusion. For example, memorization of information/facts and being able to regurgitate that information is very inductive. These facts, which could be in the form of observations, hope to inform inferences and ultimately conclusions. This is not, however, always the case.

Best of all is to use both approaches together. Writer and cyber-security expert Daniel Miessler suggests that we should be "willing to use both types of reasoning to solve problems, and know that they can often be used together cyclically as a pair, e.g., use induction to come up with a theory, and then use deduction to determine if it's actually true." [22]

I've found this to be effective in my own journey of entrepreneurship. As you know, my company, Curemark, was founded to develop a treatment for Autism. It all started with an observation I made about children with Autism and what they ate—and more importantly, didn't eat. Whereas their Autism symptoms come in many varieties and levels of severity, in all the history I took on these children, I started seeing that most of them ate exactly the same things. A pattern was glaringly obvious. Kids can often be picky eaters, but these kids pretty much ate ten things. I used to call it the "ten things diet," or the "white things diet." It got to the point where a parent would come see me with their child, and if they had Autism I would say, "I can tell you what your child eats. Waffles, chips, fries, maybe a chicken nugget, or a hot dog or pizza with a little cheese on it—and bagels, because we're in New York. But no significant protein." I wasn't right with every child, but often enough I was. Some of these kids avoided eye contact, others hated the feeling of seams in their clothing, others were distressed by loud noises, but here was one factor they shared—they would not willingly eat protein. I set out to see if I could find a physiological reason for this.

When I approached experts in the field, they said, "It's what we call 'oral haptics': they don't like the feeling of things like meat or nuts in their mouth." This didn't make any sense to me. While each child had its own version of sensory issues, why would only protein result in aversion in the mouth? I suspected that there was a problem with something physiological that tied in with their Autism and this unique self-selected dietary regime. That was the deductive part.

To determine if indeed that could be true, I had to collect data. I did an inductive process of collecting laboratory tests on the kids with Autism and compared them to children without Autism. I found a large group of the children with Autism had a specific enzyme deficiency, which is likely tied into the amount of serotonin they can manufacture in their brains during the first five years of life. In this discovery we utilized both deductive and inductive reasoning.

Our current medical science heavily utilizes inductive reasoning. Everything is done in the form of inductive experimentation and clinical trials looking for observations (outcomes) that can objectively be gathered. Gathering the correct amount of the right kind of data is key to determining if your conclusions are correct.

A   A   A   A   A

Experiment 1

ACAPPAXCATFAB

Experiment 2

One would expect that if the outcomes from Experiment 1 are all As, then A is the outcome. However, when we perform Experiment 2 and we take more data points, we can see that the answer is not at all A. This is an important aspect of collecting data: making sure that you have the right number of data points, that the question you ask to obtain that information is clear, and that it gives you the answers (outcomes) that you seek. There is a whole science around how much data to collect, how many subjects should be in a clinical trial, and so forth.

This is one of the main issues with Big Data. How much do you collect? We've seen the problem with having too little data, but even if you collect too much data, it could lead you to spurious correlations. Being able to examine the right amount of data, data that answers important questions, and looking at a good statistical analysis can help in many ways. But just collecting data for the sake of collecting data may never answer the important questions, or it may send you down a rabbit hole chasing things that are not real.

Higher order tools may not always reveal what we need to know. In orthopedics, physicians use X-rays, CT scans, and MRIs, among other diagnostic tools. However, X-rays often don't reveal what the problem is—for example, with an injury, many orthopedists skip an X-ray and go straight to an MRI. Good doctoring says that you cannot make a diagnosis from one tool; you must use more than one tool because the patient presentation (the signs or symptoms of injury, illness, or disease) is important.

One must look widely and gather all the data one can before making a determination. Recently one of the great baseball players in MLB kept having neck pain, and the public kept being told that the MRI on this player showed he had a sprain or strain, but the player wasn't getting well quickly. It was first reported that he slept wrong and had a stiff neck; then he was thought to have injured himself at the end of the prior season. It turns out they were looking for a soft tissue injury when in reality, it was a fractured rib and partially collapsed lung that were discovered months later. The doctors just needed to take a good old-fashioned X-ray that would have revealed the broken rib.

If you're looking to identify a "pain point" in your business, follow a logical progression so that you can rule out wrong answers and arrive at correct ones. Ask more questions, even if it costs you time, money, or effort to get the answers. Look widely because the answers might not be what you expect. While developing their self-driving cars, Google was very vocal about how good its vehicles were at avoiding crashes. Even so, the company knew that collisions were inevitable. One of their solutions to this issue was to file a patent for what I call a "sticky hood" (U.S. patent # 9,340,178). If a pedestrian stepped in its path, they would stick to the hood rather than hurtling across the street. "Human flypaper," some people called it. Because when you dig into the major cause of injuries when a car hits a human, it's not the impact with the car that is the main problem—it's the "secondary impact" when the pedestrian is thrown off the moving vehicle, usually hitting the car roof, another vehicle, the road, or they are run over by the car that hits them. As a representative of the American Physical Society put it, "Getting hit by a car once is much preferable to getting hit by a car and then the ground and then another car."[23]

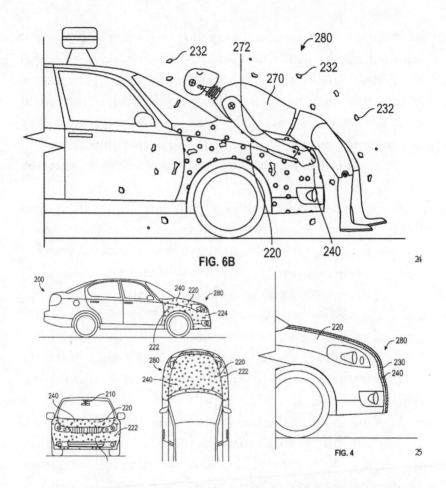

FIG. 6B

FIG. 4

Both business and medical decisions require full and detailed information *and* the capacity to interpret it. "Knowing what makes an argument sound is valuable for making decisions and understanding how the world works," writes TEDx organizer and speaker Jeremey Donovan. "It helps us to spot people who are deliberately misleading us through unsound arguments. Understanding reasoning is also helpful for avoiding fallacies and for negotiating." [26]

Treat your business decisions as diagnoses. Examine the evidence carefully and with an open mind. And don't ever settle for the kind of lopsided reasoning that only comes at a problem from one direction.

> It is wise for entrepreneurs to utilize data and both deductive and inductive reasoning to help solve problems and make decisions.

CHAPTER 8

MAKE UNCERTAINTY YOUR COMPANION

Much of the uncertainty of law is not an unfortunate accident: it is of immense social value.

—Sonia Sotomayor, Associate Justice of the Supreme Court of the United States

As we saw in chapter 1, according to Stanford's d.school model, uncertainty is the first step in design thinking. The quote beginning this chapter demonstrates that Justice Sotomayor understands uncertainty well. I believe that her appreciation for uncertainty may in part emanate from her deep love of baseball. Let me explain. Having grown up near Yankee Stadium, she is a lifelong Yankees fan. You can see her at the stadium at least once a season, sitting in the right field "Judge's Chambers" and wearing the special robes allocated to those lucky enough to snag a seat by Aaron Judge's frequent homerun location.

For baseball players, uncertainty is a constant companion. Besides the fact that when you play defense it is difficult to antici-pate where the ball may be hit, you can go 0 for 4 at the plate one day and 3 for 4 the next day. Your 3-for-4 performance may begin a ten-game hitting streak, followed by a season-long slump. Not so different from life, really.

In baseball, perfection is not the norm. A batting average over .300 out of 1.000 is considered excellent. To put that another way: getting a hit one-third of the time is considered an outstanding batting average. If you had a batting average of .333 you would be showered with accolades and hailed as a hero. In other walks of life, though, achieving your goal one-third of the time would be measured far closer to failure than to success.

Baseball players devote themselves to a game that is not one of perfection, but one where continual striving is everything. It is not just what happens on the field today, but what happens tomorrow and throughout the season. Injury, disappointment, and failure can all be a part of the game. The people who move past those obstacles with grace and grit inspire me every day.

Because baseball is not about perfection, it offers such important lessons to us as changemakers and entrepreneurs. A lack of perfec-tion is baked into the game. If players were perfect every time, it wouldn't be baseball.

Fans are not necessarily drawn to perfection or privilege, so they often root for the underdog. Things have changed in recent times, but for many years the majority of baseball players never went to college. It's not like football or basketball, where you may spend four years in college, get drafted by the NFL or NBA, and go out to play a professional sport the next day. Because it takes so long to develop the proper skills in baseball, you spend a lot of time in the minor leagues. It takes some time to develop fine baseball players. Some amazing athletes such as Michael Jordan tried to become professional baseball players, but as skilled and as athletic as Michael Jordan was, he was not going to be an A baseball player.

Change and making a mark are not related to perfection in any way. In fact, they are more akin to failure than to success.

When we undertake bold adventures, especially in business, uncertainty plays a large part in our trajectory. Somewhat different from risk, which we will examine in the next chapter, uncertainty keeps you in a constant state of flux, and presents you with a need to be flexible. As an entrepreneur and a changemaker, uncertainty is your constant companion. Never mistake it for an exception: it most certainly is the rule. If there is one thing that is sure in life, it's that you cannot be certain of what the future holds, how people will react, or whether your ventures will succeed or fail. Uncertainty is certain.

I always look at uncertainty as a commodity. Like equity, patents, and products, uncertainty is one of the many components an entrepreneur has to deal with every day. It is your business to learn how to work with uncertainty, to trade one known or unknown for another. Uncertainty is an asset. As novelist Margaret Drabble wrote, "When nothing is sure, everything is possible."

Learn how to work with uncertainty and get it on your side. I've found four ways to embrace uncertainty and to make it my friend.

1. CONTROL WHAT YOU CAN.

Baseball players know too well that you can only control how *you* play the game. You can work to hone your skills, advance your athleticism, and become an outstanding fielder and hitter. What you cannot control is where another batter hits the ball, how it bounces in the field, the playing conditions, and how your team-mates will react under certain circumstances.

Assuming nine hitters in a baseball game, the number of ways the coach can make the batting order is 9 factorial. The coach may select the leadoff batter from nine players, the second batter from the eight remaining players, and so on. The last batter will be chosen to hit ninth as he is the only remaining player not assigned a batting slot. The calculation looks like this (! is the factorial symbol):

$$9! = 9 \times 8 \times 7 \times 6 \times 5 \times 4 \times 3 \times 2 \times 1 = 362{,}880$$

This is a vast number of permutations of the players' batting order. And even that calculation does not account for stealing bases, team dynamics, bad bounces, or any other element of uncertainty that goes into the game.

Coaches control what they can; in particular, these are the batting order, the preparedness of the players with respect to prac-tice, having deep knowledge of their competitors, and encouraging good chemistry within the team.

Some of the best teams are not full of the best players. Consider the Golden State Warriors of a few years ago. The team was very talented; they dominated the NBA for over five years. They kept winning for a few reasons, not the least of which is that the team was not overburdened with big egos. Steph Curry is as willing to pass the ball as he is to hit a 3-point bucket. He and his compa-triot Klay Thompson, as the "Splash Brothers," play selfless and amazing basketball. But they have a particular chemistry that has been instrumental in their success, and it has a lot to do with their head coach, Steve Kerr. Because of who he is and how he learned to be a part of the mixture when he played for the Bulls, Kerr has the capacity to make the total outcome greater than the sum of its parts. To round out the success of the team, they played defense, had a great bench, and had an incredibly supportive front office.

The same is true for entrepreneurs. Let's say you have developed a product that does three things but does only one of them really well. An expanded need in the marketplace for a secondary aspect of what your product does, or the development of a new product by a competitor, may necessitate a shift in your product focus. You can't control the market, but you can control how you meet a marketplace need or how you pivot your product.

Control what you can and let go of what you cannot. Accept that uncertainty is a given in your life and find the points where you can limit that uncertainty.

2. DON'T BE BLINDED BY THE NUMBERS.

Like many sports, baseball has become all about analytics. Right now, there is a trend that has taken over the game called the shift, or the defensive shift. It works like this: When a power hitter comes up to the plate who, for example, "pulls the ball" to right field most of the time, the defense moves to the right side of the field to cover the areas where that batter is most likely to hit the ball. The maneuver has been around a long time, but in the past five years or so, everyone has started doing it—because analytics is king in baseball right now. But here's the thing: the statistics show that the shift works roughly half the time. The other half? It doesn't make a difference. Would the results be the same if the defense didn't shift? We don't yet fully know.

You can't analyze yourself out of uncertainty, yet people try to do it all the time. We saw it in 2020, when our political leaders continued to emphasize testing as the solution to the COVID-19 crisis, even long after the disease had spread widely throughout the nation. To be effective, testing needs to be used in conjunction with contact tracing and isolation, and it needs to be applied at the start of an outbreak when there are just a few chains of transmission. Some countries, including South Korea, were able to use testing and tracing early to control the disease and avoid mandatory lockdown measures. According to an April 2020 article by Jimmy Whitworth "identifying cases of the disease with testing did not keep pace with the geographical spread of infection around the world."[27]

In a pandemic, testing gives you data, it doesn't give you control or erase uncertainty. Acting on the data reduces uncertainty and helps solve problems.

For innovators, running the numbers is a good thing. I love seeing good data put to good use, but on the flip side I hate seeing it misused. Sometimes we get sucked into the numbers, and we are deluded into thinking we have more control than we do.

3. DON'T BE FOOLED BY YOUR OWN NARRATIVE.

A few years back, when the Yankees' Aaron Judge came up to play in the majors, he was much applauded for his amazing athleticism and his skill as a player. Standing six feet, seven inches, he works hard at his craft every day. To remain centered and focused, he keeps his 2016 rookie batting average of .179 on his phone. It reminds him of where he came from and how easy it is to slip into a horrible slump and go from the .299 to .300 he batted in his sophomore season back to .179. It keeps him humble, regardless of his performance at the previous at-bat.

As entrepreneurs and changemakers, we, too, need to be humble and not buy our own narrative. Like baseball, entrepreneurship is not about perfection, and it is not about today. It is about the journey, the season, the moments of success.

It is hard to resist buying your own narrative. A strong narrative can be highly seductive. "This is a fabulous idea, go for it!" "Don't stop now, you're just around the corner from a breakthrough!" "You're a genius, the world just needs to see it!" Oversized narratives such as these can produce complacency and a sense of entitlement that have no place in either baseball or entrepreneurship.

Let's say our product or service solves an anticipated e-commerce problem that many online retail stores are going to experience in the future, or we have a product that we have reason to believe is going to become ubiquitous in every household. These beliefs can become important focal points for our products. But the prevailing times and the prevailing markets often work against where we are and what we are trying to do. This was true for Research in Motion (RIM), the Canadian company that developed the BlackBerry range of smartphones and tablets. Once *the* device was in every executive's hand, the BlackBerry did not change with the times. The emergence of the iPhone and Android platforms led to diminishing market share for the BlackBerry. The company also struggled to attract new talent to its headquarters in Canada. The confluence of these factors sent the company—once the clear leader in the market for mobile devices with a superior product—into a downward spiral. RIM's leadership team refused to believe they would not continue to be the prevailing platform: they had bought their own narrative about how important their product was.

Complacency is a dangerous place, and it's a place to which our oversized narratives often draw us. Far better to embrace the fact that we dwell in uncertainty.

4. MEET PEOPLE WHERE THEY ARE.

Empathy—we're told that we need it, but many of us are not quite sure what it is. I am talking about empathy in this book for entrepreneurs and changemakers because we need empathy as a guide. While we lead with focus and energy, and intense concentration on our journey, we also need empathy for our peers, colleagues, and business partners, but also for those who will use our products and services. A company cannot remain viable if its CEO has lost his or her capacity to empathize. It will never create the kind of working environment where everyone can flourish. A company culture that permits prejudice, bullying, and exclusion among employees is also one that hinders a free flow of ideas and outcomes.

We get distracted by the idea of empathy as being something like sympathy, compassion, or even mind-reading. Empathy is none of these things. There is nothing sentimental about it; empathy is simply another data point that enables you to recognize the reality of your situation. It is meeting people where they are. Empathy doesn't always take us directly to a place where we know what someone is thinking, but it leads us to ask the questions we wouldn't otherwise ask. We need to remain aware of others in our lives—our employees and our customers—to make sure that we are meeting their needs on our way to success.

In the end, empathy always wins because it brings you, the entrepreneur, closer to your leadership team, your employees, and your customers.

As entrepreneurs, we need to control what we can, keep analytics in its place, not buy our own narrative, and remain empathetic.

Uncertainty is not an impediment to change. It's how you respond to uncertainty that will prove either an impediment or an asset for you.

Make uncertainty your companion. Look at uncertainty as a commodity. Like equity, patents, and products, uncertainty is one of the many components an entrepreneur has to deal with every day. It is your business to learn how to work with uncertainty, to trade one known or unknown for another.

CHAPTER 9

FALL IN LOVE WITH RISK

The world only gets better because people risk something to make it better. Thanks, Egyptians.

—Paulo Coelho, Author

I am often asked how it can be that both my brother and I are entrepreneurs, albeit at very different times in our lives and in very different fields—aerospace and biotechnology.

I believe that two aspects of our upbringing contributed to us arriving at the same place. First, we learned very early on in life that risk is not something to be afraid of. Second, we learned that solutions to problems will not always exist where others think they are.

This chapter explores the first of those two elements.

My brother and I learned to play chess as soon as we were old enough to wrap our heads around the game, at ages three and four.

In chess, you are constantly taking risks. No matter how deeply you calculate your next move, there always comes a point where you have to embrace uncertainty and make a decision. We grew up understanding risk, and that sometimes you must make yourself vulnerable to gain something of value. Chess also teaches you critical thinking skills, probability, abstract thinking, and other skills that help one manage risk.

Chess runs deep in our family culture. In fact, my parents fell in love over a folding chessboard on a commuter train, traveling daily to NYC for their respective jobs. Both were in their late twenties, and both worked in the insurance industry, though for different companies. Dad was in underwriting, while Mom worked on the actuarial side. Both ultimately worked with insurance and "large risks," as they are called in that field: Dad insured skyscrapers and the legs of famous dancers for a reinsurance firm (where multiple insurance companies take a piece of the risk), and Mom specialized first on the actuarial side and later in her career in "large lines" underwriting, working with large-scale commercial risks.

My father would often say, "Everything is insurable—you just have to assess the risk and pay a premium that covers that risk." Even more important, my parents both believed that risk, for the most part, is not random and it is calculable. It is not something to avoid. In many ways, it can be calculated, planned for, and managed. Of course, there will always be that unplanned event that happens, but that is the "gamble" of insurance.

By definition, risk is the possibility that something bad may happen. Money is lost, a vehicle breaks down, a person is injured, a team is defeated. Risk is usually associated with a negative event, but even some positive events can have risk attached. Let's say you make an investment, you take a risk, and it pays off. But now you are in a higher tax bracket. Or you win the lottery and suddenly you are elevated out of poverty but do not know how to manage the windfall. Now you can buy that house you always wanted and the car of your dreams, but there may be a price to pay. Relationships may suffer when relatives seek a handout or friends feel alienated by your newfound wealth.

Earlier I mentioned the play *Sweat*, written by Lynn Nottage, which won the 2017 Pulitzer Prize for Drama and had brief runs both on and Off-Broadway. The play is set in Reading, Pennsylvania, and it tackles multiple aspects of our society, from the cost of industrialization to race relations. *Sweat* takes a critical look at real people and how they are impacted by changing circumstances beyond their control.

When I both read and saw *Sweat*, something struck me more than any other message from the play. All the characters, save one or two, are completely unwilling to take a risk and are unwilling to embrace change. They are content to do the same jobs their parents did in the factory; they are unwilling to embrace the diversity of the plant, especially in management; and they shun the one young person who believes his only way out of Reading is to go to college. Going away to college, which for many of us is a simple and beneficial act, is looked at as a betrayal of a lifestyle, and comes with the cost of losing connections and loyalty.

We deal with risk many times every day, but for the most part we don't see these events as risks. Say the GPS in your car offers two routes to your dentist's office. One detours you from your usual route because there is an accident ahead. You balk because the route with the accident is more familiar to you and the alternate one is not. Do you risk taking the route you know well and perhaps run late for your appointment, or do you take the more unfamiliar route that is more likely to get you to your appointment on time?

Some risks are far greater than keeping your dentist waiting, and innovation brings with it some outsized risks as well as potentially colossal rewards. Putting new ideas together, creating new pathways and new tools, and employing—in some cases—unproven things in "uncharted" areas mean that one must take risks. All innovation involves risk, and the risks are as varied as the innovations.

Many of us have too singular a view of innovation; in reality, start-ups come in different forms. Each different form of innovation carries with it a specific risk. Some innovation is only a small departure from what already exists and carries less risk than something completely novel.

The archetypal start-up is what I would call a "primary start-up." It exists to commercialize novel technologies, products, or services. It sets out to fill a primary need in the world, to solve a problem that has not been solved. In some ways, these kinds of companies have become the new seats of innovation in the world today.

Surrounding the primary start-ups are large numbers of companies that exist to commercialize technologies related to the primary start-ups. These "secondary start-ups" provide products or services to support, enhance, or piggyback on a primary start-up's technology. We see this often in Silicon Valley, where a thriving start-up turned mega-company attracts other "bolt-on" start-ups. Consider the myriad advertising companies that specialize in creating ads for their clients to place on Facebook. The best of these secondary start-ups may end up being acquired by the primary company—in fact, that may be their founders' exit strategy. Facebook, for instance, acquired the animated picture platform Giphy in 2020 with the intention of integrating it into Instagram (which is, in turn, owned by Facebook).

"Tertiary start-ups" provide support or services to the primary and secondary start-ups. Software, manufacturing, or cybersecurity providers often target primary or secondary start-ups as their main source of new business. HackerOne, for instance, is a leading security platform that counts PayPal, Spotify, Twitter, Google Play, and Slack among its customers.

One final category is what I call "me-too start-ups": new ventures chasing a piece of the action established by a primary start-up. Think of Snapchat tilting at Facebook, or Lyft's face-off with Uber, and most recently, the advent of TikTok.

Innovators may be the first player on the field, but they may equally be second in line, waiting to improve upon what has just been invented or established anew. Companies such as eBay, giving rise to Amazon, and Facebook, giving rise to YouTube, Instagram, and Twitter.

Risk of failure, risk of financial disaster, risk of copycat operations, risk of going to market too soon or too late, risk of missing the boat or miscalculating the need for your invention. This is true regardless of the type of innovation you are undertaking—all new things present with their own unique set of risk factors. The type of risk and the level of risk, however, is tied to the type of innovation that is being undertaken, whether primary, secondary, tertiary, or me-too company.

If your start-up is offering something truly *de novo*, you must first demonstrate that there is a need for that thing—or you must invent the need, just as Steve Jobs did when he launched the smartphone revolution. If you are working in an established area, the risk is less because the world has already seen such a thing before. The imperative to educate, to build infrastructure, to demonstrate demand, is much less. You have a level of polling because people are already responding to your service or product. You have more information—and the more information you have, the less risk there is.

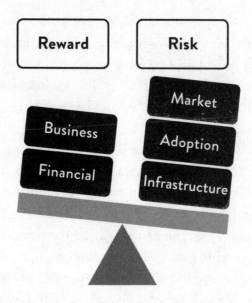

The greater the risk, the greater the reward. Creating novel technologies that solve problems can bring huge rewards, but they also bring huge risks. It was far riskier to be Mark Zuckerberg, taking on the task of creating Facebook, than to be the entrepreneur with a company that creates ads for Facebook. In the biotech world that I occupy, it is far riskier for a company to take on securing approval for a novel new drug than it is to get approval for a generic or "me-too" drug.

You see this in the treatment for Alzheimer's, where the very first early drugs were approved utilizing a specific mode of action (how the drug works), and it formed a new category of drug. Then three or four others were approved utilizing a similar mode of action and an FDA pathway that included the same or similar outcome measures. The first drug is likely to get a much larger financial reward and outcome for its investors and its creators than the ones that came later.

Bolt-on, tertiary, or me-too companies do not necessarily solve major problems. They are more likely to solve ancillary complications of accessing the primary technology, say, or offer ways to enhance the primary technology. They will be far less innovative than the primary start-up and therefore have a lower risk profile. Low-risk ventures are certainly not without reward. They can still attract high amounts of investment capital—sometimes even higher than for the primary ventures—investors appreciate that the risk is lower and the timeline to commercialization is shorter.

The company I founded, Curemark, started with something I observed about children with Autism and their dietary habits. I often heard people say, "When you meet one kid with Autism, you meet one kid with Autism." Each child has an entirely different presentation, an entirely different set of symptoms. But as I mentioned in an earlier chapter, I observed that many of these children had the same eating patterns, which led me to identify an enzyme deficiency that likely affects how children with Autism potentially make neurotransmitters in their brains.

Today virtual biotech companies are spun up out of universities every day of the week, but Curemark was one of the first. A *de novo* start-up of that kind bears the most risk of all. Think of Steve Jobs. With cofounder Steve Wozniak, he created the Apple 1, a personal computer with no monitor, no keyboard, and no mouse—at a price that put it within reach of individuals as well as corporations. Nothing like it existed at the time. Now we think it genius, but at the time, banks were reluctant to lend them money— the idea of a personal computer seemed absurd, so Apple had to prove there was a market.

Humans have long been fascinated by risky ventures, and some people will take huge risks for little reward other than bragging rights or the honor of being one of a very few to accomplish something difficult or even apparently impossible. George Mallory, a veteran of three Everest climbs, was one of the early explorers to map the Tibetan route to the summit. When asked, "Why do you climb Everest?" he famously replied, "Because it's there." He went on to say, "The first question which you will ask and which I must try to answer is this; What is the use of climbing Mount Everest? and my answer must at once be, it is no use. There is not the slightest prospect of any gain whatsoever."[28]

Yet there must be some benefit to someone, surely? Let's briefly look at the risks and rewards of climbing Mount Everest. Not being a climber, it's harder for me to anticipate the benefits ever outweighing the risks, but here we go . . .

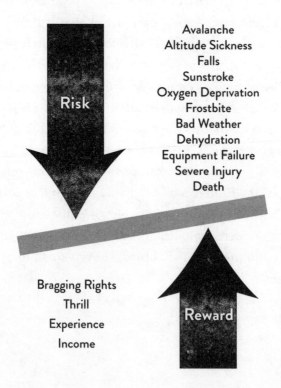

Risk

Avalanche
Altitude Sickness
Falls
Sunstroke
Oxygen Deprivation
Frostbite
Bad Weather
Dehydration
Equipment Failure
Severe Injury
Death

Bragging Rights
Thrill
Experience
Income

Reward

Risk is not random. While it can be influenced by unexpected events and fluke occurrences, risk can be measured and anticipated, for the most part. Sure, there are many aspects of the environment that can influence risk—as vast as an avalanche or as insignificant as a traffic slowdown—but these influences form a matrix that can be measured. Here is where statistics help to form the matrix of risk and can help us to better understand the risks we face. For example, looking at the number of people who have attempted to climb Mount Everest and failed will give us some idea of the risk. How many of those who attempted failed and turned around, and how many of them died trying?

We can see from the diagram on the facing page that the risks of climbing Everest far outnumber the benefits, and yet thousands of people every year try to reach the summit. In recent years, the sheer weight of traffic on the mountain has resulted in even greater risks: altitude sickness and exposure for climbers waiting their turn to attempt the narrow passes in good weather. The crowded conditions in recent years have significantly increased the chance of injury and/or death.

Some of us appear to be hardwired to seek out risk—so-called "adrenalin junkies." They race cars, they jump out of airplanes, they ski from helicopters. They constantly seek to add new activities to their repertoire of thrilling but risky things.

Those who truly don't fear risk are the exception rather than the rule, of course. What is almost universal is the tendency to gauge risk in illogical ways. After 9/11, for example, New Yorkers did not want to travel by plane because they feared another terrorist attack, so instead they drove to the places they needed to go. More cars on the road produced more accidents, as driving is inherently riskier than flying. During the COVID-19 pandemic, people didn't want to eat Chinese food because they feared that the food could carry the virus because the virus started in China. Common sense dictates that a plate of chow mein prepared in a kitchen in Minneapolis bears no direct link to mainland China.

At a casino, we calculate risk at the roulette wheel based on the number of times black comes out. When it comes out ten times in a row, we figure that red is bound to come out next. In fact, red is only "bound" to come out as much as it was during the ten previous spins. Nothing has changed in the risk, and yet we assume it has decreased. The likelihood of certain events doesn't change based on the incidence of what came before.

Sometimes we rely on social norms—the informal rules that govern behavior in groups and societies—to guide our behavior and our assessment of risk. We assume that people will adhere to the established way of doing things. The Trump presidency taught us that our assumptions of how our leaders will behave can't be relied upon. They are not embedded in law or guaranteed to protect us. Trump's desire for power and notoriety far outweighed his respect for historical precedent or cultural norms. A 2017 *New York Times* article observed, "Trump's flouting of norms was the siren song of his candidacy, and it has become a defining feature of his presidency. Along the way, he has exposed flaws in the structure of American governance that haven't surfaced in modern times, mainly because no other president has probed them."[29] Political, social, and economic norms were not challenged in any big way by one individual until the Trump presidency.

The Trump presidency also demonstrated another minefield in managing risk, which is the use of flawed logic. In 2020 the Trump administration decried the use of testing for COVID-19. In a June 15 tweet, then-President Trump said testing "makes us look bad." At a campaign rally in Tulsa five days later, he said he had asked his "people" to "slow the testing down, please." At a White House press conference, the following month, he told reporters, "When you test, you create cases."[30] The math doesn't quite work that way, however. It is true that expanded testing will reveal more positive cases. However, more testing does not create more cases nor account for an increase in the positivity rate. A higher positivity rate amid expanded testing is the only statistic that reflects the virus spreading through a testing area.

Not knowing that something exists does not make it not exist.

We saw a lot of flawed logic and magical thinking through the pandemic in 2020. Humans are such emotional beings, and wishful thinking and deflection of reality were rife. As the British newspaper *The Guardian* noted, from overpromising on testing to inflated expectations for a vaccine, "realism is in short supply."[31] In addition, politicians' desire to emphasize the upside due to a mixture of spin and natural—even desperate—optimism, scientists and researchers were under intense pressure to succeed in research, generate good publicity, and win additional funding. But flawed or even fraudulent logic and a leadership that shirks the truth cannot lead to any kind of accurate risk assessment.

In baseball, risk is just the flip side of opportunity. A team can "bank" skills to take some of the risk off the table. If you've got a player with outstanding speed, they will run the bases fast and that will reduce some risk there. If you've got a rock-solid catcher behind the plate, you reduce the risk some more. A good manager whittles away at the risk to increase the opportunity to win. The use of data and analytics has transformed the game of baseball in the last few years. Shifts placing fielders in places where batters are statistically likely to hit the ball are now commonplace. Putting one player in over another could have everything to do with how well that player hits against right-handed or left-handed pitching, or how well that batter has hit against a particular pitcher in the past. MLB teams have expanded their analytics departments, and they appear to grow every year. Some have begun to push back against the analytics in some ways. For example, if a certain player does well against a certain pitcher, the manager is likely to want to play that matchup. However, the batter is just getting over the flu, and maybe isn't 100 percent. Do you go with the analytics or the manager's knowledge of the player's condition?

Excelling at sports or business requires a high level of "risk intelligence": the ability to accurately estimate probability. While many factors will always be uncertain—how well the other team will perform on Saturday, what the market will do next month—we can make educated guesses based on even the limited information we have available. Most people are unskilled at estimating probabilities, but author and risk expert Dylan Evans found: "Occasional islands of high risk intelligence in odd places...among horse-race handicappers, bridge players, weather forecasters, and expert gamblers." In the case of gamblers, Evans noted that, "The expert gambler makes money and the problem gambler loses it. But there are emotional differences. Although they both gamble a lot and it appears to be compulsive, expert gamblers know when not to bet, they evaluate their opportunity each time." [32] Again, we see statistics playing a role in evaluating risk.

Evans believes that we are not stuck with the risk intelligence we were born with. Instead, we can build it by being aware of our own cognitive biases. "Expert gamblers are constantly on the lookout for overconfidence, biases and so on. It is hard work, but it means they know themselves pretty well and they don't have illusions. They know their weaknesses." [33]

For me, risk is something to be assessed and managed, not feared. I don't go looking for risk, but neither do I shy away from it. Strange to say, but avoiding risk carries its own form of danger.

Playing it safe with a bolt-on innovation that relies on an established product can mean that you risk missing the moment or being redundant. Today change occurs rapidly and often, and timing is everything. Build the product that was needed four years ago, and the outcome will likely be failure.

In true entrepreneurship, there will always be risk. Without taking chances, a start-up will not grow.

Taking chances in business and in life is a little like playing a sport. Before you step on the field, you must be in condition so you are prepared to enter the game and physically able to play. And then to play well, you need to embrace every aspect of the game: offense, defense, and knowing your opponent's weaknesses and strengths as well as your own.

For innovators and change agents, risk is part of the landscape, but remember that all risk can be measured within a reasonable set of parameters. When we undertake a novel project or an endeavor intended to make change, we humans often assess risk using flawed logic, or choose high-risk activities with little reward. Choose your risks wisely, know your own biases, and calculate the consequences. Risk, after all, is never random.

In true entrepreneurship, there will always be risk. Without taking chances, a start-up will not grow. Avoiding risk carries its own form of danger. Playing it safe can mean that you risk missing the moment or being redundant.

Today change occurs rapidly and often, and timing is everything. Build the product that was needed four years ago, and the outcome will likely be failure.

CHAPTER 10

OWN YOUR MISTAKES— AND DON'T LET THEM BECOME FAILURES

The price of greatness is responsibility.

—Winston Churchill

One of the things that I believe is dwindling in our digital and social media age is accountability. When I was growing up, it was deeply important to take responsibility for what you did, to be accountable to others and to yourself. Whether it was for an action you took, a score you received on a test, or how you chose to treat someone, taking responsibility was something that mattered.

As an entrepreneur or changemaker, mistakes are inevitable. They are learning tools, much the same way we saw in chapter 1 about design thinking, and how iteration and prototyping are key. Without iteration or prototyping, which allows for "learning mistakes," we could not develop our innovation properly. Mistakes are incremental. They can accrete and combine and blossom into a failure if you don't acknowledge them and take responsibility for them. Own your mistakes; don't let them become your failures.

Now, we regularly struggle with the question of who should take responsibility for all kinds of things. San Francisco-based psychologist Samantha Smithstein says, "This seems to be a constant issue in American society: the question of where corporate or government responsibility ends and personal responsibility begins. Did McDonald's make coffee too hot, or is burning yourself a possible hazard of drinking a hot beverage? Should we be forced to wear seatbelts, or should death or disability be the price you pay for choosing not to?"[34]

When we remain accountable for our actions, we are taking responsibility for how our actions affect ourselves and others. During the pandemic, refusing to wear a mask could put yourself at risk, but it put others at risk too. While we may think about those with whom we come into contact and how our lack of mask-wearing could put those people in jeopardy, it goes well beyond that. If someone gets sick because of our disregard for their safety by not wearing a mask, this newly passed-on illness may impact many, many more individuals beyond just the one directly infected person.

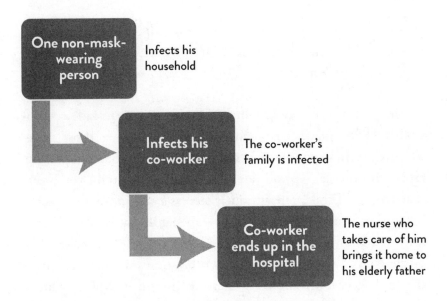

For one non-mask-wearing individual, and assuming four people in a household, upward of twelve people could become infected by the actions of one person not wearing a mask. Recent data from the NFL season mapped the transmission of the virus on the teams. According to a *Wall Street Journal* article, the NFL managed to play a sufficient amount of the games to call it a full season, but what they learned along the way is fascinating. The league mapped the genetic material of the virus when it was detected so they knew exactly how it was transmitted. They determined that transmission for the most part did not take place on the field, as mainly the fields were open and contact with others was short and not sustained. But they did find the following:

- The virus traveled beyond six feet especially in small, poorly ventilated areas.
- Masks mattered more than the duration of contact.

- Cumulative brief interactions exceeding fifteen minutes could lead to transmission. It did not have to be fifteen consecutive minutes.[35]

This was a new way in which the NFL began to take responsibility for its players. For entrepreneurs, as well as those of us who are just living our lives, responsibility makes for an important aspect of growth. We will not always choose the right path, and that's okay. Mistakes are uniquely necessary in entrepreneurship because it is a setting that calls for significant trial-and-error learning. Sometimes we head into the wrong space or make a key mistake in what we are doing, and other times we make precisely the right decisions. There's no getting around it. Mistakes are a necessary part of becoming a successful entrepreneur.

Taking responsibility for our mistakes is not at all the same as beating ourselves up or plunging into a place of shame. Neither of those responses is productive. We own our mistakes, but they do not own us.

When we do not take responsibility for the mistakes we make, we place ourselves in a position of blame and deflection. We are robbed of the opportunity to move into a place of learning and examining. As we will explore more fully in chapter 15, self-belief allows us to receive mistakes as a meaningful teacher. The lessons we learn from our mistakes are so valuable and so key that they can keep us from making even larger mistakes down the road.

In a world where everyone gets a trophy, we are neglecting to teach our children that failure is a normal part of life. If you are raised to expect external acknowledgement and praise after every test, race, or game, the absence of that feedback impairs your life. That's what narcissism is all about—craving feedback from the outside because your inside is empty.

Back in chapter 6, I told the story of hearing Shaquille O'Neal and Billie Jean King speak about their upbringing. They both shared one thing in common. In both cases, their parents never asked them after a match whether they won. They wanted to know how they played.

Catastrophic failure—such as when a plane crashes—generally comes from a series of back-to-back mistakes when a premise is bad and each next step is the wrong one. Mistakes and failures are not the same thing. We will always make wrong choices, and we will always do things that are not correct—those are mistakes. When there is a goal we are trying to achieve or machinery we are trying to perfect, we can fail to reach the goal or fail to get the machine to work. Failures are sometimes the result of mistakes, but not always. You will recall the "clumping drug" we discussed in chapter 2. The manufacturing team made a mistake putting hot materials into a foil bag when the material was still a few hundred degrees in temperature. That mistake led to a failure of that batch to become a usable one.

I often make a point of distinguishing between issues and problems. I tell my team that we can always deal with issues. No matter what we do, issues will inevitably come up—we make mistakes, others present challenges, but if you don't tell me what the issues are and we don't expose them, that's when they become a problem. Before you know it, that problem has become an impediment that keeps us from going in a new direction or seeking our desired outcome. The way I see it, the issue is two steps short of being a problem and you can take action to prevent it going those extra two steps. Keep it an issue; don't let it become a problem. Bringing the issues out into the open early will allow the greatest amount of time for resolution.

As a physician, I always took responsibility for my mistakes—I'm thinking here of errors of judgement or anticipation, or reaching the wrong conclusion based on the facts before me. I believe mistakes most often come from not asking the right questions and not probing a situation to the fullest extent. Again, bringing as much light to a situation will allow you to make the correct decision. If you are diagnosing a patient and you jump to a conclusion about a symptom they are experiencing, you can reach a conclusion that may or may not be catastrophic. That is why medical diagnoses are never made—or should never be made—based upon the analysis of one modality. Looking at a blood test may tell you something about the body, but without another mode of examination it is difficult to get to the right conclusion. That is why physicians are always told not to treat their own family and close friends as they potentially could abdicate their objectivity, especially when something catastrophic is present. The same is true in business—moving ahead too quickly without compiling all the relevant information may lead you into the wrong market at the wrong time or run you up against unanticipated logistical barriers.

When we give away our power and shift blame to others instead of accepting responsibility for our own actions, we make a very large mistake. Sometimes we allow others to steer us away from taking responsibility; they help us shift blame in other directions. There will be times for you as an innovator and as a human being during which a colleague, an investor, or even a trusted friend will try to convince you to do something that is not exactly the right thing for you or for the company. The action they're suggesting might be acceptable today, but it may have long-standing consequences that are not part of your desired calculation.

By handing responsibility for your actions to other people, you can find yourself pulled into a place you don't want to be. I liken it to being pulled down into a well. It takes far less force for someone to pull you into that hole in the ground than for you to get yourself out again. From physics, we know that pushing a cart involves more friction than pulling a cart. Being pulled into a place you do not want to go will end badly when you want to extricate yourself. The sheer effort required to get out is a bear— and on the way back out, gravity is not in your favor.

In business you might make a decision because you were hauled into a space. You needed money, it looked like an attractive deal, or you expected a group of investors would bring particular assets to the table. You're sucked in, and then when you want out, it's not going to be easy. You're going to get scraped and scratched extricating yourself from the well.

When you find yourself under pressure to take a step in your business, consider this: if it doesn't work out, what will be the blowback? If you have to climb back out of that space, what kind of detrimental consequences might you encounter? I have this conversation with my lawyers all the time. Most often it starts because I want to pursue a course of action that is not customary.

"That's not how it's usually done," they tell me.

"Well, first of all, can we do it this other way, and what are the consequences?" I respond. "If we do it this new way, I believe it will speed up the process and give us maximum flexibility. What do you believe will be the long-term consequences, if any?"

I certainly have pushed the lawyers to look at doing things in different ways. And while I must say our lawyers are very conservative and very excellent, I give them new ways to look at things all the time.

For business leaders and changemakers, the consequences of an apparently harmless and novel choice can be profound. I was asked to advise a professional athlete on the wisdom of endorsing a certain pharmaceutical product. I'm not a big believer in celebrities promoting drugs unless they themselves have the condition it treats. Golfer Phil Mickelson has worked on public awareness campaigns for plaque psoriasis, and tennis player Venus Williams has been open about having Sjögren's syndrome, an autoimmune disease. In my mind, having a disease makes an individual a much better spokesperson for a condition and for a drug they use.

I'm reassured that this particular athlete has an excellent team of advisers to guide him, but in this case as in all cases, the Peter Parker principle prevails: "With great power comes great responsibility." Although the phrasing became popular through Spiderman and the late, great Stan Lee, the concept has been around since at least the 18th century. A collection of decrees by the French National Convention in 1793 included these words: "*Ils doivent envisager qu'une grande responsabilité est la suite inséparable d'un grand pouvoir,*" which can be translated as "They must consider that great responsibility follows inseparably from great power."[36] Winston Churchill said much the same, in the quote at the beginning of this chapter.

I take the view that if you are going to promote a drug and be the spokesperson for it, you need to know what side effects it may create. What are you endorsing and what potential problems could it bring to those who use it? Sometimes these issues are unknown or not predictable, but doing a deep dive into what you are promoting is crucial.

Superheroes or not, all people—especially those of true authority—need to take responsibility for the consequences of their actions. By owning your mistakes, you will not let them turn into your failures.

> For business leaders and changemakers, the consequences of an apparently harmless choice can be profound.
> When we take responsibility and remain accountable for our actions, we are taking responsibility for how our actions affect ourselves and others.

CHAPTER 11

MAKE TRUST YOUR BEDROCK

He who does not trust enough, will not be trusted.

—LAO TZU, ANCIENT CHINESE PHILOSOPHER

I thought I knew all there was to know about trust.

I always trusted my family to have my back. My parents would always back my brother and me in doing the things we wanted to do. Mom and Dad would tell us, "Whatever it is you want to do, we'll help you in the best way we can."

My patients trusted me with their healthcare. These young children understood that I would always be there for them, and that I would always tell them the truth. Their parents knew I would not mince words, nor would I ever give up on them. They trusted that if they had a problem that I could not help them with, I would always say to them, "I may not know what's wrong, but I will 'dog it to death' with you until we do find out together."

I trusted my friends. I have a friend I met in Latin class when I was fourteen and we have been best friends ever since, for the last forty-five years, always making sure that two weeks do not go by before one of us reaches out to the other. I have new friends in my life whom I also trust to turn up for me.

It wasn't until I started Curemark that I realized how much trust belongs in business. I originally thought that trust was something that you had in your personal life, with family and friends. What I came to realize is that trust belongs everywhere—it is the bedrock upon which we live. When I started my company, I learned from one of the "masters" about trust in business—specifically about "brand trust" and the fact that empathy is inextricably bound to trust and to success.

Loreen Babcock, who is currently vice president and chief marketing officer at Montefiore Health System in NYC, was one of the originators of the concept of "brand trust." She is responsible for the award-winning movie *Corazon*, a true story about a young woman's encounter with a Montefiore Einstein Center cardiologist in Santo Domingo who ultimately saved her life. Loreen was also instrumental in creating a wonderful video tribute to the frontline healthcare workers who valiantly fought the COVID-19 pandemic, which was aired on many channels.

When I first met Loreen, she was the CEO at her own agency called Unit 7. Loreen spent most of her career in healthcare advertising and branding, but her twist on all of it was (surprise!) that healthcare is about the *patient* and the patient's needs. It is about empathy. Loreen had a chief trust officer in her organization long before the concept of trust was visibly promoted in many organizations. When I first met her, she was coming off a month-long branding exercise with her team. She had decided that the best way for her team to understand the drug she was branding for diabetes was to understand the diabetic patient. And the best way to understand that patient, she believed, was to become one. So she and her whole team took on the role of a diabetes patient for more than thirty days. They altered their diets, they took time away from what they were doing to simulate the time it took to give oneself a shot of insulin, and they monitored their sugar levels multiple times a day.

Loreen understands empathy and the need to have empathy at the center of a brand. Products that solve a problem for patients can only be effective with deep understanding on the part of the organization and trust on the part of the patients. "Brand trust," the term she coined, emerged as a concept in advertising and has never left.

Just as products need trust, so should trust be at the center of each of our personal "brands." Trust in our mission, our word, and our focus. Trust in one another.

Fairness, empathy, and trust go together. Recently it became apparent that one of our vendors at Curemark had to go way beyond the requirements of our contract in order to accomplish the goals we had set in the original contract. So while in small measure we have made up some of that ground and shared in some of the expense, my sense of fairness—but even more, my sense of collegiality—prevailed. I went to my board and told them that I would like to give this vendor more money, and they agreed. They agreed because they know that partnerships require trust and fairness for them to be effective.

As we discussed in chapter 3 with respect to DEI, in their book *Unleashed*, Frei and Morriss speak to the topics of trust, leadership, DEI (diversity, equity, and inclusion), and empowering others as core to the future of effective business—and moreover, core to empowering leadership. Frei and Morriss have a premise that I think is deeply important: "We think about trust as rare and precious, and yet it is the basis for almost everything we do as a civilized society."

Among other things, they describe the three "core competencies" of empowerment leadership as *trust, love,* and *belonging.* In laying this groundwork, they clear the path to understanding that leadership is not about the leader, but rather about others. Leadership of this kind is built on a bed of trust.

If you are looking for a prescriptive way to find empowering leadership, I suggest you read their book.

Racial injustice, the lack of DEI in the workplace, and the structural racism (both explicit and implicit) that exist in our society are all based on a fundamental lack of trust. The failure to arrive at equitable change for true inclusion and for reform is based on an ongoing lack of trust. It is not remotely surprising that people of color exhibit a lack of trust due to their historical and continued treatment. That treatment ranges from the historical roots of slavery to the experimentation on Blacks, such as the highly unethical "Tuskegee Study of Untreated Syphilis in the Negro Male," which ran for more than four decades, the racial disparities in the criminal justice system, and the ongoing exclusion of people of color from clinical trials—there are so many examples, it would take far more than this book to list them.

Tina Opie is an associate professor in the management division at Babson College, currently MIT's MLK visiting scholar, and CEO of Opie Consulting Group, which advises well-known organizations on DEI strategies. When asked why organizations are slow to incorporate DEI strategies, Opie responded, "Many white people think they're going to have to give up something, and they don't want to do that. That's why they treat diversity like an add-on, not as an essential element of their organization, because if they really believed in it . . . we could change the culture of an organization in six months if we put money, effort, and time behind it."[37]

What we see here is an inherent lack of trust on both sides. POC see their exclusion in the loss of a multitude of social, emotional, economic, educational, and other opportunities afforded their white counterparts, and it is a loss they experience every day. Meanwhile, White people are desperately afraid of losing their privilege and the opportunities that have been afforded them since the founding of this country.

The truth, I believe, is that White people lose nothing as a result of DEI. To the contrary, everyone gains. Talent is spread widely, and as we read earlier, having diverse talent makes tremendous sense for any organization. Including people with diverse points of view only enriches an organization. Instead of spending so much time and energy trying to suppress voting—which is a fundamental right in this country—encouraging every American to exercise their civic duty and vote for representation should be encouraged. Our elected officials should look like us.

Without a basic sense of trust, none of what we have spoken about in this book can really work. Somewhere along the way, the lack of trust catches up with your personal journey or your business one.

Fairness and empathy and trust go together.

Racial injustice, the lack of DEI in the workplace, and the structural explicit and implicit racism that exist are based on a fundamental lack of trust. The inability to achieve equitable change, true inclusion, and reform is based on an ongoing lack of trust.

Remember trust belongs everywhere: it is the bedrock upon which we live.

SECTION 3

MAKING CHANGE HAPPEN

WHAT ALL OF US CAN DO,
INDIVIDUALLY AND COLLECTIVELY,
TO CHANGE THE WORLD

CHAPTER 12

BEND, DON'T BREAK

Flexibility is the key to stability.

—JOHN WOODEN, AMERICAN BASKETBALL COACH AND PLAYER

Becoming an entrepreneur at age fifty meant that the way I interacted with others was firmly entrenched. Years of clinical practice had built my empathy and my humanity so that they became my calling card. Moving from clinical practice to a start-up necessitated learning and growing personally. It taught me extreme flexibility, a keen ability to pivot, and a constant hunger to move my company forward. Darrell Rigby and his coauthors in *Doing Agile Right* emphasize: "The best predictor of a successful hunt is not a cheetah's top speed; rather, it's how fast it stops and turns." [38]

"Our world is going through quantum leaps in change on all levels and in every sphere, and such changes affect each of us differently. Some of us will welcome a specific change with open arms, while others will see that same change as a threat. Our economy is chameleon-like, our modes of communication now would have been unthinkable fifty years ago—maybe even five years ago. In order to survive such twists and turns, it is clear that we must remain flexible.

The one imperative for start-ups of all kinds—and for all of us who are trying to effectuate change, whether in our business or in our personal lives—is to remain flexible. We may not achieve the highest speeds in our area of influence, but we can always be ready to pivot.

Retail tells this story very clearly. Brick-and-mortar stores, which once thrived on foot traffic walking through their doors, no longer achieve most of their sales through face-to-face inter-actions. Online stores, and sites such as Amazon—where all types of merchandise can be found in one place—have begun to predominate in the U.S., just as they have in China and elsewhere across the globe. The retail companies that have stuck with one mode of sales and haven't read the change in consumer behavior or proved themselves capable of flexibility are now at risk of cata-strophic failure. Take a look at Toys "R" Us, Brookstone, David's Bridal, Barney's, RadioShack, and Sports Authority. All were once mainstays of the retail landscape, yet all have gone under, or been subsumed by other companies. Their brick-and-mortar stores now house other businesses or have a "For Lease" sign hanging on the front door. Or take Sears—they were originally a catalog company before adapting to a brick-and-mortar presence. Sears was flexible enough to move from catalog to brick and mortar but could not bend the other way when the time came. Giant SEARS letters lean, unwanted, against storefronts. "Store Closing" banners adorn last-day Sears stores across the nation. As a society we have substituted speed and instant gratification for the touch and feel of the retail experience. Amazon, eBay, and other online retailers enable the consumer to choose widely. Whereas when you go to a store that has a limited footprint, choosing from a small selection no longer feels advantageous nor wanted.

Even more businesses did not survive the changes in eating, buying, and travel habits that were forced upon us by the COVID-19 pandemic. The businesses that thrived were made to be flexible and could survive change; others were in the right place at the right time. Timing is everything. For example, in a culture where SoulCycle spinning classes had taken over a significant portion of the urban exercise world, outside of multipurpose gyms, they could not in some cities survive the pandemic. The classes embodied all the conditions that could potentially spread the virus: close quarters, flying sweat, poor ventilation. SoulCycle's closest competitor, Peloton, where the instruction was remote and could be accessed from one's home Peloton bike, became the go-to exercise for the "spinning crowd." At one point there was a backlog of months if you wanted to buy a Peloton to exercise at home. SoulCycle adapted its bike and classes to an at-home version, but Peleton was already way out ahead, so SoulCycle pivoted again and brought classes outdoors.

During the pandemic, restaurants were faced with multiple challenges: loss of business, laying off trusted employees, and the food insecurity that many urban dwellers faced. So many restaurants became inventive and exhibited tremendous flexibility in the face of these challenges. Many instituted robust take-out and delivery businesses, switching in many cases entirely from in-restaurant dining to take-out. They found ways to institute outdoor dining in the absence of in-restaurant seating, which was restricted in various states. They tried hard to keep their employees engaged and working, and many tended to the needs of their fellow community dwellers to provide meals where major food insecurity existed.

The *Oxford English Dictionary* defines flexibility in three ways:

1. The quality of bending easily without breaking.
2. The ability to be easily modified.
3. Willingness to change or compromise.

Ever found yourself walking along and see someone wearing headphones coming toward you? They are locked in their music or their phone call or their podcast, oblivious to the world around them. As the other person comes closer, you know you will have to swerve around them. They aren't going to change direction, and you're on a collision course. When you are so concentrated on one thing, you can't be flexible because you're not even aware that you must redirect your path. It's the same in business and in life—trying to bend from a place of singular focus is extremely difficult.

I often find myself acting as a judge at shark tanks, where entrepreneurs showcase their company or technology in hopes of receiving funding. The kind of shark tank I generally participate in is not as fierce as you see on TV. Springboard Enterprises runs a version called a dolphin tank, which is intended to teach participants all about entrepreneurship. Similarly, Barnard College has a summer program for high school students where they spend ten days in New York City and visit start-ups. At the end of the ten days, they have a "Pitchfest" where the students are given five minutes to sell their business idea to the panel. It's a simulated session, and the intention is to help the participants learn rather than crush them in front of others.

Sharks and dolphins alike, the most common mistake I see founders make is managing their company to a specific exit. This is a strategy that comes out of the venture capital model, where investors want to put their money to work for X amount of time. After that, they need an exit—or to put it another way, a vehicle to recoup their investment, such as the sale of the company or a public market offering such as a listing on a stock exchange (IPO). Investors want liquidity. Entrepreneurs have come to see the exit as the outcome, rather than building a sustainable business for the long-term.

Let's take Company A run by Mr. Entrepreneur—we'll call him Mr. E. for short. He has a unique technology that treats atrial fibrillation (AF), a type of heart arrhythmia. He decides to raise 20 to 25 percent of the total funding he requires for clinical trials so he can provide sufficient proof of concept data to support not the full approval, but "just enough" to be acquired. Knowing that Biosense, Webster, and Medtronics are major players in the AF market, Mr. E. tells investors that his company will likely be acquired by one of these two companies in eighteen to twenty-four months after proof of concept, or after limited clinical trials. This very specific exit strategy has little to no built-in flexibility. It doesn't leave room for things that cannot be controlled, such as these companies developing similar technology on their own or moving out of the AF market. Not only that, the presumption of a timed acquisition in the very early stages, and even further down the road, doesn't account for proof-of-concept failure, the need for additional funding, or any other hiccups. And believe me, hiccups *always* happen.

It's true that investors need an "exit." But managing a start-up to a predetermined exit too early ignores the significant risk it creates for the investors, as well as for the technology itself.

When I started my own company, I really wasn't thinking this way. To be honest with you, I was pretty clueless about how investors thought. I did know that in biotech you had a longer runway. Clinical trials are long and expensive, and even if they are successful, they are subject to regulatory scrutiny. Once I realized that, I could see that I needed to stand by my product and our work as we prepared not only to see the drug through the clinical trials and eventual approval, but also through early sales of the product. Having this strategy enabled us to be as flexible as possible and to enjoy the ability to exit or to build a company. I learned in my years of practice that children who had a global delay, where multiple domains of their development lagged behind, had a potential for a good outcome—their prognosis could be good if they continued to make progress across the multiple domains. If a child lagged severely behind in one domain and did not make progress in that domain, their prognosis was not good. This is how I look at business and, especially, my own company. Making sure that all the domains remain in continual progress is key to success; making sure that the financial, the intellectual property, the clinical, and other domains all progress simultaneously.

Holding on to any concept too hard can lead you to failure. In an increasingly complex business world where we must often tap into seemingly disparate concepts or perspectives, being too "one-minded" will put you at a disadvantage when you need to pivot or change your strategy.

Through my years as an entrepreneur, the single most important thing I have learned is that entrepreneurship is a personal journey, one that involves—even requires—tremendous growth.

Entrepreneurship, leadership, and personal growth are intricately intertwined. For my company to grow, scale, and be successful, I, too, must be ready to grow, scale, and be successful. Without this kind of personal change on the part of the founder, the business invariably gets stuck, one way or another. The price of rigidity is failure.

If we go back to that dictionary definition of flexibility and examine it carefully, you will see that each of its three qualities is vital to start-ups. They're the backbone of the advice I give to entrepreneurs daily:

1. Be able to bend without breaking. Practice what I call "corporate yoga."
2. Design your technology, product, or service to be easily modified (in terms of time, cash, and focus).
3. Have a willingness to change course—or to compromise with the marketplace, investors, and suppliers—to achieve your objectives.

I look at it this way: If you take a piece of spaghetti that's not cooked and you try to bend it, it snaps. If you take one that's fully cooked and you bend it, it just flops around. If you take a piece of spaghetti that's in between—the *al dente* state that Italian cooks say is just right—it is in a place between rigidity and flip-flopping all over the place. Flip-flopping is as bad as rigidity in my view. Sending your team in multiple directions because you are flip-flopping or holding fast in the wake of needed change sends equivocal messages to your team, as well as to your audience.

This flexibility I'm talking about is not about being overly malleable and changing direction at the drop of a hat, but rather having a thoughtful understanding of the landscape around you and a willingness to pivot if necessary. My experience in business is that nothing is forever. No does not mean *no*, it means *not now*. Things may seem bad and dire, yet tomorrow they can turn around. So hold your needs and your position strong, but practice corporate yoga so that you are able to bend, but not break.

Every January I head south to Florida to play baseball. I take part in a camp hosted by the Yankees, where you get to be coached by, and play with, former Yankees Major Leaguers. Generally, it's me along with about 150 guys.

I'm of an age where I never got to play typical hardball as a kid. I played sandlot ball, and I played with the guys on the block, but I never faced hardball pitching. I played fast pitch and slow pitch softball my whole life, but never saw live hardball pitching. The first time I went to one of these Yankees camps, a former Yankees pitcher who is noted for his curveball threw me one. My friend Ken had told me beforehand, "Just remember he's going to throw them in the dirt, so don't chase it." Then to make sure I understood what I was going to be facing, he added, "Hopefully you'll be able to see it coming..."

I have never experienced anything like it. The pitcher threw the ball and it was like a huge beach ball coming right at me. It was going around 80 miles per hour, but at least I could still see it. I could see the red seams rotating, so I got a sense from them of the trajectory of the pitch. Standing in the batter's box, I finally got it. You have to be able to follow the trajectory, using calculus to figure out in your brain where that ball is going to travel. You have to start swinging literally when that ball leaves the pitcher's hand.

When you're standing at home plate and facing the pitcher, the trajectory of a ball is deceptive. It makes a big arc, so you can easily swing at the ball and miss. But if you look carefully at that ball as it's coming toward you, the red seams on the ball reveal to you the trajectory. Each curveball has a specific rotation, so watching it closely will enable you to decide whether to hit it or let it bounce in the dirt. Life will always throw you a curveball, and you need to be ready for it.

Just like cheetahs getting faster, pitchers are now able to throw the ball harder and faster than ever before. The median pitch has become almost one mile per hour faster over the past decade, and "many more pitches are hitting 100 mph."[39] In life and business, too, pitches are coming at us faster than ever, so it's even more imperative to flex and pivot.

When we prejudge circumstances or situations, we can be caught out and find ourselves in a stance from which we can't pivot. Flexibility is our friend at times like these. By not setting our hearts on a specific outcome, we set ourselves up for the ultimate best outcome, both in business and in life.

> Holding a concept too tightly can lead you to failure. In an increasingly complex business world where we must often tap into seemingly disparate concepts or perspectives, being too "one-minded" will put you at a disadvantage when you need to pivot or change your strategy.

CHAPTER 13

DON'T HIDE WHO YOU ARE

To wear your heart on your sleeve isn't a very good plan;
you should wear it inside, where it functions best.

—MARGARET THATCHER, BRITISH PRIME MINISTER 1979–1990

One of the hardest things in life, I believe, is to be authentic. We so often fear revealing our true self, or we have simply become so adept at hiding our true self that we no longer are in touch with ourselves.

"Just be yourself," we are told again and again. It may seem like a self-help cliché with no logic behind it—except that there are pragmatic reasons to follow this advice. The bottom line is this: it is *hard not* to be yourself. It takes tremendous energy—physical, emotional, and psychic—to hide who you are. The hiding lies in the world of sociopathy and narcissism, not in the world of wholeness and balance.

We have a paradox, then. It's hard to be yourself, but it's even harder *not* to be yourself.

So while this is true, we also live with another paradox, which is that while everyone is looking for the next best thing, very few people are willing to take a chance on it. No one ever was fired for too much conventionality. But for too much risk, too much change, too much deviation from the norm? People do get fired for that, especially in large organizations. This is why it is difficult to stand up and stand out.

Let's untangle that first paradox by first considering what it means to "be yourself," or to be authentic. *The Merriam-Webster Dictionary* offers this definition of *authentic*: "true to one's own personality, spirit, or character." Think about what that means for you. It means you can turn up in a business meeting as fair-minded, or witty, or Ecuadorian, or female. You don't have to pretend to be brutal, or humorless, or Boston-born and bred, or one of the guys.

Our personal identity is made up of many facets. You may be a witty Ecuadorian female engineer who excels at mathematics, is an introvert, and enjoys the theatre. All of those things may be true of you at the same time. You may be a female Caucasian nurse who has an amazing singing voice, is a mom, has six siblings, and likes to play competitive badminton. These various parts of ourselves make us who we are: multidimensional.

Being yourself need not mean being one-dimensional, but rather living in all parts of yourself. It means embracing all the aspects of your character. Graceful and gritty, tough and tender, compassionate and commonsensical—all of us have different facets, and it is most authentic to acknowledge the complexity that lies within us. Sometimes we find that others try to make us one- or two-dimensional so that they can categorize us and place us in a box. Sometimes it is easier to conform to what others think about us than to be who we are.

Here, I think of Margaret Thatcher, who served as the British prime minister from 1979 to 1990. She was made of many elements and was not afraid of revealing them when they needed to surface. She was many things: a chemist, a lawyer, a wife, a mother, a politician. Authentic to the last, Margaret Thatcher was certainly not universally admired. As Britain's first female prime minister she met a lot of opposition, she held some of the lowest approval ratings of any British prime minister, she had a unique ability to enrage people, but she was highly respected. By being herself, she was able to concentrate all her energy into leading the nation in the way she believed was best for its people.

She held seemingly disparate and competing views. For example, while she was a leader who believed in the privatization of state-owned utilities and was mostly against trade unions, which she felt harmed the workers, she was also one of the first leaders of any nation to call for climate protection and the preservation of the ozone layer. She was against apartheid but refused to support sanctions against South Africa. She recognized that as the proud people of Britain became more of a minority, they would react poorly to an influx of immigrants, even if they added to the "richness of British culture," so she opposed immigration at various points in her tenure.

Thatcher had a rare ability to couple her strong religious upbringing with her scientific background and environmentalist convictions. Thatcher remained true to her principles throughout her service as prime minister and never shrank from conflict. Even as Britain was swept by a devastating recession, riots, homelessness, and poverty, she famously declared that she was "not for turning." To her, consensus was merely "the process of abandoning all beliefs, principles, values, and policies in search of something in which no one believes, but to which no one objects; the process of avoiding the very issues that have to be solved, merely because you cannot get agreement on the way ahead."[40]

Changemakers of all kinds attain maximum influence by exercising deep and sincere authenticity. We can accomplish far more when we are authentic than when we are not. When we are authentic, we can be stronger and, at the same time, more flexible.

Often founders believe they must adopt a veneer that does not reflect who they are, but demonstrates toughness, aloofness, or some other characteristic that prompts others to see them as a true leader. They do it out of a feeling that this is what needs to be done, what has worked before, so they also must do it. In the corporate world, many people think you have to be tough, rude, and obnoxious anytime someone is not doing what you want them to do. I believe otherwise. I have had to say no, stand firm, and call people out plenty of times, and I have found ways to do it without being an asshole. I have chosen to make those moments teachable ones rather than ones that engender shame. In chapter 16, we will look at shame in detail and how it can ruin a company to have a leader who lives in shame or employs shaming tactics.

Oftentimes a "founder identity" gets so far removed from the true person that the founder ends up acting as something akin to a double agent. Undercover agents are experts at leading a double life, but it comes at an immense psychological cost. "When a person passes classified information to an enemy, he or she initiates a clandestine second identity," explains CIA clinical psychologist Dr. Ursula Wilder. "From that time on, a separation must be maintained between the person's secret 'spy' identity, with its clandestine activities, and the 'non-spy' public self. The covert activities inescapably exert a powerful influence on the

person's overt life. They necessitate ongoing efforts at conceal-
ment, compartmentation, and deception of those not witting of
the espionage, which includes almost everyone in the spy's life.
For some people, sustaining such a double identity is exciting and
desirable; for others, it is draining and stressful."[41]

One of the harshest criticisms that people in business can face
is that they are not tough enough. The message seems to be that
business leaders need to be harsh or bullies or crass or a whole lot
of other negative qualities. It's a viewpoint that implies business is
a harsh, oppressive, crass place, and you must bring all the negative aspects of your behavior to the forefront to succeed.

Women hear this all the time.

In the early days of building my business, not too many weeks
passed by without someone speaking to me as if I were incapable
of understanding the complexities of the business world, or even
my own technology.

Aside from generally being the only woman in the room, I
was often the only one new to the business world, navigating a
landscape that is dotted with sharks, naysayers, and cynics—all of
whom want and hope to make money from you and your invention but are deeply skeptical that they can. The paradox always
amazed me, and it still does to this day.

In addition to the inventor start-up skepticism, there is also a
gender piece. In those early days, some bankers were more apt to
kick off a meeting by addressing my male intern rather than me.
Frankly, it didn't matter what was being discussed—the likelihood
of me being recognized in the meeting as the principle rather than
as an ancillary was far too low for my liking.

In one meeting with a banker, who was also the parent of
a child with Autism, and his wife, who wished to be present, I
was halfway through my presentation when he interrupted me
and said, "Who do you think you are, to invent this? Brilliant

minds have been tackling this for a long while, and you think you can just come along and propose something that could work for these kids?"

My response was, "Yes and oh, wow. I guess we're done here." I walked right out of that meeting, right out the door.

Another time, many years ago, I was in a meeting with my board where a banker was making a statement about future valuations. When I questioned how he came up with his calculations, as it differed from previous ones, he said to me, "Don't worry, Joan, you will get your horse farm in Bedford." It was a euphemism: all little girls dream about riding horses, and in this part of the country, Bedford is the place for it. It was probably the most condescending thing anyone has ever said to me. After my board member reamed him out about his remark and my harsh, and totally not shy, language about who he thought he was to speak to me that way, he soon left the firm. I am sure I am not the only person he spoke to in that manner.

Thank god this doesn't happen anymore. At the time, though, all the introductions in the world did not seem to make it go away, so I needed to figure out why they treated me that way and how to fix it.

One day when I was just sick over one more meeting and one more snub, I happened to be having dinner with my brother. I asked him, "What the heck is going on with this, Jay? They treat me like a little girl, they address things to the intern, and somehow they're not getting that I am the inventor and the founder and CEO of the company."

My brother is two years younger than I am and my only sibling. We are two very different people, with differing sensibilities, but we have a shared understanding of the world as it presents to us. When we were kids, I always had to pick him for my team because

he was not the best athlete. He was happy to be soldering components in his room while I was out playing basketball or baseball.
Jay never had to study to get good grades; I had to study long and
hard. He was an entrepreneur very early in his career; I was an
entrepreneur very late in mine. He sees the glass half empty; I see
it half full. Jay has a brilliant, brilliant mind, but never wanted
to teach. I love to share knowledge with other people. We're very
different people, with very different ways of being, but now we
work together at my company every day, and I value his perspective more than almost anyone I know.

So naturally, I asked Jay what the heck was going on. "Joan,"
he laughed, "it's simple—they're mistaking your kindness for
weakness. You are warm and collegial, not at all what they are
accustomed to. You present a very welcoming front. You're a
newbie entrepreneur without business experience, so they assume
you are naive and ripe to be exploited."

"What is it about my behavior that makes people think I'm not
tough enough, or not a good businesswoman? Why do people
make assumptions like that?" I asked Jay.

"You smile," he said simply. "You are one of the happiest people
I have ever met, even in the face of adversity or stressful, tough
times. You are totally in touch with what is happening, and yet
you manage to smile. Not everyone is capable of that, and people
don't always understand it."

He went on, "You dress professionally, but not in a suit. Your
clothes have a softness to them, and other people don't know how
to read that." It's true that I've never gone for the "woman suit"
look. I favor Eileen Fisher with flats over power suits with heels.

There was more. "You hug people," Jay pointed out. "People
don't hug each other in business. But you hug everyone, and they
don't know what to do with that." For the record, I don't go around

hugging total strangers. Even so, I've often been in a place where I hug someone I know and someone watching will say, "Hey, can I get one of those?" I admit it: I am a hugger.

Jay said, "You listen to people. You are far more likely to listen to what others have to say or ask questions of them *before* you open your mouth. Most of the time people are trying to sell something or bully others into agreement. You just don't do that."

"There's one last thing," Jay told me. "You don't brag. You tend not to speak about yourself or your accomplishments, of which you have many. Most people in business have accomplished far less than you have and yet they will talk about what they have done ten times more—in some cases, incessantly."

"People don't know what to make of you," Jay explained to me as we finished our meal. "And because businesspeople do not like uncertainty, they put you in a box." Most of them, he surmised, would say one of the following:

- She hugs people, so she mustn't be very tough.
- She doesn't talk about her accomplishments, so she probably doesn't have many.
- She smiles a lot, so she is more heart than brain or brawn.
- She is letting me talk, so there must be some deficiency or weakness there.
- She is not saying much, so she probably has little to say.

It all made sense when he put it that way. But I was still frustrated: How could I overcome all these preconceptions without becoming someone I'm not?

"Use the element of surprise," Jay advised me. "They may think you are a pushover, but when the time is right, shove back *hard*. They will get that you're not a pushover. Whatever diminishing comments they make, let it all roll off your skin like you've got a Teflon coating. That will put them in a place where the box they put you in will not be the correct one and watching them do the 'box scramble' will be quite something. Remember, Joan, they don't like uncertainty, but uncertainty is where you live, it's where you thrive. The strategic advantage is yours."

This was one of the best lessons in life I have learned. Because it worked. When investors met me with condescension, I pushed back. That meeting with the bankers and the line about buying a horse farm? When the meeting ended, I pulled that banker aside. "You will *never* fucking talk to me that way again. Ever. I am done with you. What would ever make you think you could say that to me, especially in front of my board?"

Jay ended our conversation with the following advice, which has proved to be a fundamental lesson for me, one I have shared with founders and women in business for almost ten years now:

"Never let anyone mistake your kindness for weakness."

I believe this is not only a lesson for founders and women, but for all young people or newbies at anything. And it goes even wider than that. Anyone who faces what may look like an imbalance of power or knowledge or feels intimidated because they think they don't know enough, or they aren't strong enough—if that is you, then you should take this lesson to heart. I have expanded the advice to make it even clearer and more sweeping:

"Don't let anyone mistake your kindness for weakness: not on the playing field, not in a negotiation, not in the boardroom, not anywhere, or at any time."

Using the element of surprise that Jay spoke of can come in handy, especially when you can get people to look beyond their own thoughts. In 2020, I was umpiring a charity softball game at Yankee

Stadium for the NY Yankees Foundation and CC Sabathia's PitCCh In Foundation to help inner-city youth. CC and his wife, Amber, are just stellar people, and they do important work for children across the U.S., especially in the Bronx and northern California.

One team was led by Michael Strahan, the football star turned TV host, and the other was led by CC himself. Both teams were packed full of all kinds of celebrities, film stars, and sports stars. I was positioned behind home plate when suddenly Michael came out of the visitors' dugout waving a bat at me.

He held it out to me and said, "The pine tar is too high—there is way too much pine tar on the bat. This is illegal, and I think you should recall the last hit from Leslie Jones."

With that, CC came bounding out of the home dugout, having overheard our discussion.

You might recall the story of George Brett, who in 1983 hit a home run for the Kansas City Royals in a playoff game against the NY Yankees. The Yankees manager complained the pine tar—also known as the "sticky stuff" that helps improve the hitter's grip so the bat doesn't go flying out of their hands—was too high on Brett's bat, exceeding the 18-inch limitation. Brett was accused of cheating and had his home run taken away from him.

So CC came over and he started arguing: "No it is *not*! That pine tar is just fine." They started an argument, pushing and pulling the bat, pointing to the pine tar over and over again.

Now, these are two very, very tall, big men, and they're facing off against each other with me sandwiched in the middle. This is not a fun place to be. They screamed at each other for a long while, until finally I looked up at them and in my loudest voice I shouted, "Wait a minute!" Michael and CC just stopped dead and stared down at me (literally, because I'm a foot and some inches shorter than either of them).

"Who the fuck puts pine tar on a metal bat?" I asked.

With that, they both just lost it. They could not stop laughing; I had diffused a situation that started out as a friendly staged argument, but in their competitiveness escalated.

"Go back to your dugouts and let's play this game!" I told them both.

Because I'm so affable, they weren't expecting me to curse or call them out. I took them off guard and totally took the wind out of their "argument sails." That's the element of surprise; I used it to my advantage! Try it sometime; it can be highly effective.

As I said earlier in this chapter, it is exhausting to conceal who you are. Especially as you climb the ladder in the business world, or as you begin to get traction as an entrepreneur, you have to "hide" from more and more people. You are constantly on guard, and that is draining—both physically and emotionally. Such hypervigilance taps out our reserves of 5-Hydroxytryptophan—commonly known as 5-HTP—which is a compound made naturally in the body. This 5-HTP compound assists the production of serotonin, "a neurotransmitter that plays a key role in regulating mood and sleep-wake cycles. Healthy levels of serotonin contribute to a positive mood and outlook." [42]

Scanning constantly for threats leads to an unending, low-level anxiety, which fuels a state of apprehension, says Kevin LaBar, a professor of psychology and neuroscience at Duke University. This anxiety, in turn, triggers the release of stress hormones such as cortisol, which fuels anxiety in an unending cycle. It's a vicious cycle that triggers a number of neurological, biological, and psychological mechanisms which, in turn, affect our perceptions and impair our decision-making capabilities. [43]

My parents both had tremendous integrity. Not in a showy way, but quietly. They always did the right thing when they could, even when they were going against the current of what other people around us were doing. They were authentic regardless of the circumstances. My mom recently died, and at her funeral people whom I had never met told me stories about how her wisdom and insight helped them do the right thing, when they were sandwiched between competing thoughts and cognitive dissonance.

When I was growing up, we lived in a part of the country where there was no city garbage pickup; you had to pay for private carting. Most of our neighbors took their garbage to a relative's house in town to avoid paying the carting fees. I remember my father saying to me, "That's not what you do in this world. You don't give your garbage to someone else's city. Those people pay taxes to the city so that their garbage can be picked up; we do not. We chose to live somewhere that doesn't have city pickup, so we deal with that by paying for private carting."

Many years ago, long after my father died, one of his friends came to see me in my office. We sat down and he said to me, "I have a form of dementia that is setting in, and my memory gets more and more cloudy with each day that goes by. I need to tell you something about your dad before it is forgotten."

My father's friend said to me, "My dad died years ago, when you kids were small. He lived in Oklahoma, and I couldn't afford either to go there or to bury him. Your dad bought me a plane ticket, gave me his credit card to pay for the funeral, and slipped money in my pocket that he was sure I'd need for the trip. I thought you should know that about your dad. Now just the three of us know."

My mother placed a lot of value on self-sufficiency and being responsible. A woman who worked for her was always short of money at the end of the pay period, so she would come to my mother to borrow money. After a few months of this, my mother said to her, "You know what? I'm going to take this money and put it in an envelope in the bottom of my desk drawer. If you need it, take it. Then if you pay it back, it'll be there the next time you need it." That was her way of living out her values in every facet of her life.

It is so easy to talk about authenticity like it's a soft value, a soft asset—nice to have but it does not benefit you in any way. In fact, we can choose to be authentic for very practical reasons. We saw earlier that being true to yourself uses less energy than putting on a façade, leaving you free to focus on what matters most to you: your new venture or making a difference in the world. Simply put, you will get more done by being yourself.

Being true to yourself is not complicated. It's most often the simplest way of being, but we often learn at a young age to hide what we feel both physically and emotionally.

I believe we are born authentic, ready and able to tell the truth, but our honesty gets eroded and chipped away over time by the environmental factors of our lives. Being honest, stating our truth, and resisting the mimicking that we are sometimes prone to do in order to fit in is so important to our future. At first it may seem difficult and frightening to be authentic, but in my experience, just being yourself will ultimately bring you to the best outcome with the least effort.

It takes tremendous energy—physical, emotional, and psychic—to hide who you are. Being true to yourself uses less energy than putting on a façade, leaving you free to focus on what matters most to you: your new venture or making a difference in the world.

And of course, don't let anyone mistake your kindness for weakness.

> Not on the playing field.
> Not in a negotiation.
> Not in the boardroom.
> Not anywhere.
> Not EVER.

CHAPTER 14

BANISH SHAME FROM YOUR BUSINESS

Shame is the most powerful, master emotion.
It's the fear that we're not good enough.
—Dr. Brené Brown, Author

I have seen shame defined in many ways and in many contexts. But I like to look at it as a powerful set of negative emotions that is fueled by self-consciousness or a negative self-evaluation. While driving an individual to deny, hide, or obfuscate a negative aspect of themselves, shame triggers distress, a fear of exposure or vulnerability, and a sense of worthlessness or powerlessness. To me, what is most unique about shame is that it will often reveal itself in ways that are not always associated with the source of the shame.

Central to shame, I believe, is a directly proportional obsession with self. An individual ends up spending a disproportionate amount of time and energy on the act of hiding some negative aspect they perceive in themselves. It creates a narcissistic tendency, or even results in or because of inherent narcissism.

Shame is different from guilt. Guilt is about behavior—a feeling of having done something wrong or against one's values. Shame is an internalized feeling of being exposed and humiliated. Shame is the voice that says, "I *am* bad" versus, "I *did* something bad."[44]

There is no upside to shame. Once you have been humiliated, you can carry that humiliation in perpetuity. It does you no good. I believe it is essential to find shame, get to know it, and put it in its place in your life.

Some of the most powerful works I have read during my own journey in entrepreneurship and self-growth have been about shame. Dr. Brené Brown burst onto the personal development scene in 2010 with her TED Talks about shame and vulnerability.[45] Through her many publications, podcasts, and public appearances, Dr. Brown has proven herself one of the most effective analysts of the currency of shame in our time. Books such as Andrew P. Morrison's *Shame: The Underside of Narcissism* and R. D. Laing's *The Politics of Experience* have also added to my understanding of the power of shame in our lives.

In her TED Talk "Listening to Shame," Dr. Brown explained that shame thrives in judgement, silence, and secrecy. Therefore, openness, understanding, and a willingness to be vulnerable drive out shame from our lives. She stated:

Empathy is the antidote to shame.

As Dr. Brown goes on to say, where there is empathy there is vulnerability, and where there is vulnerability, we find "the birthplace of innovation, creativity, and change." So we can see that shame and innovation are inextricably linked.

Vulnerability is often associated with failure, which we've seen is a friend to entrepreneurs and changemakers. Many individuals are not at all able to accept failure in their lives. The narcissist, for example, will turn their failures into yours, and their miscalculations into a turn of events in their environment—an initiative collapsed because of "unexpected changes," they will tell you. Never accepting responsibility, the narcissist continues to deflect any and all accountability.

While labeled "radical" in the 1960s, R. D. Laing's books offer valuable reading for 21st-century entrepreneurs, as well as for modern parents trying to understand their own behaviors as well as those of their children. Laing is best known for his work on schizophrenia, but I've learned much from the "Us and Them" theories he promoted. In his tiny but powerful book *The Politics of Experience*, Laing claims we connect with others by forming an Us mentality where a nexus of kinship is formed. In doing so, however, the nexus necessarily excludes others (Them). By forming these nexuses, we create antagonistic relationships with Them. Quickly the Us group transcends the individuals that compose it and takes on a life of its own.

The Us factor can be seen as a closed system that perpetuates shameful behaviors. Laing's model applies equally to organizations, which, after all, are groups of people in the same way that a family is. Many of the same dynamics apply.

Laing based his observations on the fact that some families (and organizations) perceive the outside world as hostile, and therefore the family (or organization) must be protected at any cost. The stability of the nexus, he argued, is everything. Within the family there is reciprocal concern and mutual protection, but most importantly, each member is expected to control and be controlled by the others in the group. This interdependence can and should be used to ward off the hostile outside world, but instead it perpetuates shame and the shaming behaviors many of us grew up with.

Business is full of narcissists—or at least, individuals who exhibit narcissistic behaviors. I had never encountered so many people cut from the same cloth as I did when I entered the business world.

People use that term loosely, but according the the Mayo Clinic, the narcissist "has an inflated sense of their own importance, a deep need for excessive attention and admiration, troubled relationships, and a lack of empathy for others." [46] They may model "narcissistic injury," for instance, by reacting negatively to criticism, boundaries placed on them, or attempts to hold them accountable for their harmful behavior.

A narcissist will lure you in and then spit you out. They are very sophisticated in how they operate, so it's not always apparent what's at play. These people often reach high levels of power in business and government because they can be very charming and charismatic. The Oval Office and other top political positions have accommodated more than one narcissist over the years.

Narcissists target people and make them feel inadequate. Their weapon of choice is *shame*.

The business world is crowded with individuals who are focused on making money, and that singular focus can make for the driving force of their work life. Don't get me wrong, there are great people in business, too, and I believe that many are interested in service and other aspects of making money, but much of business is motivated solely by making money.

In the start-up culture, success is highly prized, and company founders are often elevated to mythical stature. For successful founders the amount of money made is tremendous, almost beyond imagination. But with that mythic status comes a great fear of failure and the shame that comes with perceived or actual failure. Start-ups are inherently risky, and failure is one of the best teachers. Indeed, as we saw earlier, iterations of ideas and products are part of the development process. You can make fifty iterations of a product, but only one can be the final one. You could say all the other iterations failed to make the final cut. Certainly, there is no shame in the iteration, but when revealed outside of the company, great shame can come from that disclosure.

What can result from this fear of failure, the revelation of failure, and the shame that can come with it are behaviors that Laing spoke to. The cycle of shame becomes rampant, and it ultimately becomes the entrepreneur's worst enemy of success.

If you are someone who carries shame or have been a victim of shaming behaviors, the likelihood that you can combat a narcissistic culture, or an individual narcissist, is small. The "cycle of shame" is self-fulfilling and becomes a constant in your life. There are many versions of this cycle, which is also linked to depression and addiction. Here is one depiction:

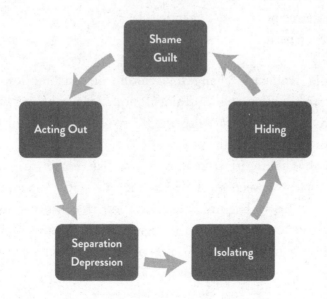

It works like this. Someone says something to you that makes you ashamed. For example, "Oh, so I hear you grew up poor and your family had no education." You can either wear that as a badge of what you have overcome, or you can make it a shameful revelation. If shameful, you begin to hide and isolate yourself from other people—people who you don't want to know about those humble beginnings. This could draw you into depression. To try to regulate your painful feelings, you act out by doing something outrageous, such as drinking too much or driving recklessly. Now you have reinforced the shame, and the cycle begins again. Around and around you go. The cycle keeps feeding itself, never stopping.

The hiding, isolation, and acting out can take many forms, and founders can easily be put into a situation of reacting to shame. When they do, these are the kinds of acting out we may see:

- Hiding and isolating
- Controlling employees and other behaviors
- Use of demeaning tactics
- Use of coercion
- Sexual or other harassment
- Systemic racial and/or gender bias
- Pay disparity

In our eminently changeable culture of consumption, fascination with technology, and globalization, never before has the entrepreneurial start-up culture been so welcomed—and yet at the same time so vilified.

Running southeast from the city of San Francisco, a valley carves a path between the East Bay foothills and the Santa Cruz mountains. At the beginning of the twentieth century, mile after mile of fruit orchards filled the region known as the "Valley of Heart's Delight." By the beginning of the twenty-first century, it was far more widely known as Silicon Valley. The orchards were, for the most part, replaced by office complexes occupied by feisty start-ups and monolithic tech giants alongside the retail and residential buildings for the population who feeds the heart of tech.

While desperately trying to rehabilitate itself with philanthropy and a modicum of ethics, Silicon Valley has taken the place of Wall Street as a symbol for underregulated, overly powerful companies filled with arrogant geniuses and entitled, young, mostly White men who show little regard for the community outside their door. Part of that arrogance is tied to the disruption of what has "always been" and fuels innovation by changing everything—from that which is old and needed to go, to that which we hold dear, such as responsibility and accountability to others.

Stereotypes, of course, are not always true. Not every start-up is born in California—far from it. A start-up may come in the form of a Silicon Valley robotics disruptor, but it's equally likely to be a SafeMotos, the on-demand transport start-up in Rwanda; a MeQasa, an online real estate marketplace in Ghana; or a solo woman in India building an as yet unsung internet venture. Even so, we hear about the "bro" culture and "groupthink" pervading start-up land, especially in Silicon Valley and the venture capital world. Those kinds of attitudes are more akin to those of cult leaders than business leaders. The organizations where these attitudes prevail are fueled by historical shame and dedicated to protecting an asset or assets at all costs. Those assets may include intellectual property, the market share, the culture, or anything that is deemed proprietary. The mechanisms used to protect those assets often include immature or shaming behaviors, coercion, and control. These behaviors can pervade the entire organization, usually emanating from the top down, while investors often remain ignorant of reckless acting out and other behaviors. It is a culture driven by secrecy that thrives on the notion that protecting the start-up is paramount so as not to suffer an attack from the outside in the form of demeaning, devaluing, or stealing information.

In recent years we have seen an entire political party living in fear of this type of behavior, which in our current climate is often delivered in the form of a tweet. Demeaning tweets have made even seasoned politicians duck and run for cover. Many people have become so fearful of this bullying behavior that they have become paralyzed with fear, unable to fight back even when they know that the tweet is a form of projection, a cover for self-loathing on the part of the tweeter. Once a party member steps out of line, they live in fear of the devaluing tweet. They fear the shame of being called out.

Happily, though, there is a way to overcome all of this: self-awareness, introspection, and empathy.

A closed system—the Us nexus of cults and bro culture—breeds shame, but an open system—characterized by vulnerability and empathy—drives out shame from our lives.

I could go into an entire treatise on narcissism and shame, but suffice it to say, when you first meet someone who is clearly narcissistic and you must interact with them, it will feel as if they have flipped your world around in bizarre ways, none of which is good. It took me quite a long time to understand and recognize the mechanism and behavior of narcissists, but once I did, they became predictable. The most predictable of all ways in which narcissists behave is that they will never stop defending themselves, warding off any hints of slight or snubs or disregard. Their ego and sense of self are so fragile that they cannot take criticism, either real or perceived. The narcissist believes that they are special, and while their bravado is beyond measure, their core is empty. They are like a leaky bucket—regardless of what praise or kindness or compliments you give them, it all leaks out the bottom. They have no ability to contain them.

The term "agent of change" is a well-worn moniker. It is used so often because in change there is a level of self-reflection and self-agency. To make change, we must first change ourselves. The capacity for personal change is something an entrepreneur, a politician, and anyone seeking to make a mark in the world must possess.

Shame—either within oneself or in others—can become a huge impediment to change. Shame can derail an entire organization; important observations and conversations are deferred because they trigger shame in us. Self-awareness, introspection, and empathy are key to breaking down shame—in us as individuals and within the organizations that we build.

> It is so important to encourage participation by nurturing self-acknowledgement and internal motivation. This roots out the formation of shame.

CHAPTER 15

OWN YOUR IDEAS AS INTELLECTUAL PROPERTY

As we enjoy great advantages from the inventions of others, we should be glad of an opportunity to serve others by an invention of ours; and this we should do freely and generously.

—BENJAMIN FRANKLIN, FOUNDING FATHER OF THE UNITED STATES

It started as an exercise in nostalgia. I would look through the patent archives in search of my favorite childhood toys. A little digging revealed Lincoln Logs, US Patent #1,351,086; the hula hoop, US Patent #3,079,728; Scrabble, US Patent #2,752,158. It was fun for me to share the illustrations on social media so others could get the same nostalgia kick. (If you're interested, on www.

USPTO.gov you can see every kind of patent, dating from 1790 to the present day.)

At first it was a walk down memory lane, but it turned into a lesson on how novel ideas, designs, and innovations become commercial assets. While these iconic toys were a part of my childhood, they also represented the business of selling toys. What these toys all had in common was that they started as ideas that their inventors or companies deemed important enough to turn into patents.

If you look at my tweets or Instagram posts, you'll see that I have also posted more recent patent illustrations. I've posted the "wrap-around screen" seen in one of Apple's patents and the Google patent for a "sticky car hood" that we discussed in chapter 7. In retrospect, Lincoln Logs and the hula hoop seem like cool ideas, but a sticky hood? A wraparound screen? They seem positively futuristic—or in some cases, quite simplistic. But all of them are ideas that could become unique products—but more than that, significant business assets.

The protection of ideas, designs, and innovation takes many forms, including patents, trademarks, copyrights, and trade secrets. Apple, Google, and most of the other big technology corporations spend hundreds of millions of dollars every year to protect their ideas and their innovations.

Our forefathers thought highly enough of patents and intellectual property to embed them into the United States Constitution. In the Patent and Copyright Clause (Article I Section 8 Clause 8) it states that: [The Congress shall have power] "To promote the progress of science and useful arts, by securing for limited times to authors and inventors the exclusive right to their respective writings and discoveries." The tradition of protecting ideas and inventions began with the Constitution and was fortified by George Washington, when in 1790 the first Patent and Copyright Acts were passed by Congress.

You could say that innovation and change are now, and always have been, fundamental to the American way of life.

Title 35 of the United States Code states that *any* person who "invents or discovers any new and useful process, machine, manufacture, or composition of matter, or any new and useful improvement thereof, may obtain a patent." Think of your patent as a fence around your property, or a claim staked in the goldfields. Patents are not granted for the ability to do something, but rather to keep others from doing or making what you have invented and invested in. It is not a right to sell or make or distribute an item, but rather a right to exclude others from using, selling, or making the patented invention or design.

Before I moved into the world of business, I didn't understand how important it was to own intellectual property. It was my brother who raised the issue with me the very first time I talked with him about the treatment I was developing that would eventually lead me to found Curemark. Back when I was still doing the early clinical trials, I was at a family dinner and my brother said to me, "So, what's new?"

"Well," I told him, "I found this really intriguing thing happening with kids with Autism and their enzyme levels."

I explained my research to him, and he said, "Well, do you think you could do something about that? Develop some kind of treatment that would fix their enzyme levels?"

"I have no idea," I replied.

"Well, I think you should patent it."

"Patent it? Why would I do that?"

"Because if it doesn't have a monetary value, no one's going to pay attention to it," he replied.

I was still shaking my head a little, but he said, "I'll have my patent attorney call you in the morning."

And he did. "Your brother writes his own patent Specification and I do the claims," the attorney told me. "I'll send you some patents in the biotech area; you start writing."

So I did. We submitted that patent application in December 1999. Today, I have about 300 patents worldwide, which is a very unusual position—especially for a woman.

Curemark, like almost all other start-ups, has transitioned through a process of discovery, validation, and scale. We would not exist as a company today if it were not for our intellectual property protection. Our IP has allowed us to protect our findings, raise money, demonstrate efficacy, and develop science that, hopefully, will benefit millions of children worldwide.

In the past decade or two, awareness of IP and copyright has become much more acute. Especially in the arena of invention and innovation, it is critical. Yet it's often the last thing an entrepreneur will attend to—because it's expensive. The filing fee is relatively small, but having the patent written can cost anywhere between $7,000 to $20,000. And then you can't stop at just one, because a patent only covers a very specific aspect of a product. In the biotech space, one patent might cover the formulation, while another covers its use. And then you have to consider the international aspect: Japan, for instance, may require a whole other set of documents. If you're going to patent in Russia, you need to have the patent translated into Russian. And on it goes, taking a great deal of energy and expertise, as well as money. This is why many founders forego that aspect and focus on developing the concept. But I urge founders to do both in parallel. Under U.S. patent law, you must file your application within twelve months of the first offer to sell your invention, or within twelve months of your first public use or disclosure of it.

Not every start-up, entrepreneurial venture, or business generates vast quantities of intellectual property, and some sectors lend themselves to protecting intellectual property more than others. But regardless of what business you are in, the first major decision you should make when starting out is determining how to protect your ideas. Here's why:

- To afford protection from others coming into your area of invention.
- To provide business protection and increase market share.
- To provide protection from copycats and counterfeits.
- To create a tangible asset.
- Patent rights can be monetized—especially important when the entrepreneur needs to raise capital.
- Patents are published in the public domain, and these innovations can spur more new ideas and innovation.

Great ideas are ones that solve problems. Protecting those ideas so they can mature for the benefit of others is key when we consider the growth and scalability of small business. One of the hallmarks of small and start-up businesses is that they often aspire to be larger ones. They want to have the kind of economic and social impact that is the backbone of job creation, economic independence, and prosperity.

The benefits of claiming ownership of your innovation are not just for individual businesses, but for the wider economy. Through their research, the Global Intellectual Property Center (GIPC) of the U.S. Chamber of Commerce has found that "Strong intellectual property (IP) protections lead to innovative new discoveries that fuel economic growth and build stronger communities. Workers directly and indirectly connected to these advancements make up a significant percentage of each state's workforce, are paid higher than their counterparts in non-IP intensive companies, and help increase the state's exports."[47]

The GIPC also points out that intellectual property makes families safer by not allowing unsafe copycat household goods to enter our homes. IP is good not only for our own businesses, but it's good for our society as a whole. Indeed, the GIPC's motto of Jobs, Innovation, Safety, and Access sums up why IP should be considered in any business as a way of creating, protecting, and monetizing an asset, while at the same time creating, encouraging, and participating in innovation.

Whether you are in a mature business or a fledgling start-up, do not forget about IP. IP builds value, creates protection, and gives back over and over again.

On the face of it, the patent process is one of the most egalitarian in our country. Patents are granted without regard for race, age, gender, socioeconomics, education, geography, or even living status—because, yes, even a deceased person can be granted a patent if their heirs apply for one.

The U.S. Patent Act of 1790 created the ability for anyone, regardless of age or gender, to protect an invention with a patent. The first woman to obtain a patent was Mary Kies. On May 5, 1809, she received a patent for the method of weaving silk and straw together for a hat. But while Kies's patent would keep others from selling hats like hers, she could not own her patent—or receive the money from the sales of her hats. Even though the patent office allowed "any person or persons" to obtain a patent, Mary could not benefit from hers due to the existence of coverture.

Under coverture, a woman had no individual legal or economic rights. Coverture laws stipulated that women were the property of their husbands and did not have a separate legal or financial existence. Women could not own property or goods or enter into contracts. This was true in the U.S. until approximately 1845, when New York State allowed women to own their patents and the money derived through their patents. This New York law was the first instance in the U.S. where women were allowed their own economy.

This stands in clear contrast to many other countries in the world such as Sweden, France, and Spain, which historically granted levels of allowance for women to participate in business. Even Russia granted women the right to a separate economy in 1753, long before Maine in 1824 allowed women to own and manage property when their spouse was incapacitated.

Despite the inability for women to own, commercialize, or to receive value from their patents they still could be granted one, thus rewarding their innovation and creativity equally despite the presence of coverture. A patent therefore promoted *in theory* the potential for equal economic status to an idea or invention regardless of gender. The patent laws of our country granted women inventorship, but the coverture laws would not grant them ownership.

Women were not the only ones barred from obtaining a patent. Slaves were often prolific inventors yet had no access to the patent system. Often their owners profited from their inventions. Freed black men, such as Thomas Jennings, did have access. He patented dry cleaning.

While the ability to be granted a patent is egalitarian, there still exists great disparity in the ability for women, people of color, and other disenfranchised groups to successfully access the system of intellectual property protections we have in the U.S. As the U.S.

Patent Office issued its 10 millionth patent in 2020, one thing has changed little since the republic's early days: Almost all of the patents go to men. A 2012 study by the National Bureau of Economic Research found that just 7.5 percent of patents were granted to women, and that just 5.5 percent of patents commercialized or licensed were done so by women.[48]

"I was shocked when I first learned how infrequently women patent," says Jennifer Hunt, a Rutgers University economist who led the study. "We are clearly not managing to put a large fraction of the population in a position to innovate."[49]

If women patent far less than their male counterparts, does this mean that women are less inventive? I don't think so. I believe that women do not necessarily think of their inventiveness as commercial.

The patenting gap is often attributed to a lack of women in STEM, but Hunt and her team argue that this fact only explains a portion of the gap. Using data from the 2003 National Survey of College Graduates (NSCG), they examined both the numbers of patents granted to men and women and the number of licensed or sold patents (commercialized) by gender and degree. They concluded: Only 7 percent of the gap in patenting rates is accounted for by women's lower probability of holding any science or engineering degree, because women with such a degree are scarcely more likely to patent than women without."[50]

And it is hurting the U.S. economy. The National Bureau of Economic Research makes the case that if the patenting gap was closed just between men and women it would result in an increase in GDP of 2.7 percent.[51] A 2.7 percent increase in per capita GDP could dramatically change our trade deficit, quality of life, and the overall world economy.

Further research shows that there is a racial and socioeconomic patenting disparity as well, where children in the top 1 percent of income distribution are ten times more likely to be inventors than children with below-median-income parents. We also know that children exposed to innovation are more likely to be inventors, and where they live influences that exposure.[52]

A 2013 Brookings Institute report stated that the one hundred largest metro areas represent 65 percent of the U.S. population but accommodate 82 percent of the inventors granted patents since 2005.[53] While metro locations appear to drive patenting, a deep need for innovation and patents exists in rural and manufacturing communities.

We need to educate women, people of color, and rural communities about the market value of their ideas and research. Taking ownership in the form of patents and other IP is not yet embedded in our DNA. It takes longer than a hundred years to overcome prevailing ways of thinking and being. But embracing their creativity and inventiveness—and their ownership of their fruits—is key not only for women and other marginalized groups to attain greater parity, but also to spur on the economy as a whole.

Closing the patent gap will not be accomplished in a day. I argue it needs to be a cultural shift in which women not only embrace their creativity, but the commercial viability and need for their inventiveness. It starts by teaching our young women that their ideas are important and have significance in society. Makers of change can have immense impact through the Ideas Economy.

I have long proposed the creation of multiagency entities in the U.S. to promote patenting and intellectual property ownership. Indeed, I testified in front of Congress in 2018 about this patenting disparity. Some of those proposed changes I would encourage are as follows.

EDUCATION

The intellectual property protections available to inventors should be taught at all levels of our educational system. The Department of Education, SBA, USPTO, and other agencies should be intimately involved with this initiative. The encouragement of women, people of color, and other disenfranchised people to enter STEM fields is currently underway at multiple levels of our society. But education in STEM alone will not close the patenting gap. Awareness and understanding of the intellectual property rights along with a STEM education should be afforded to everyone who needs or wants one and should begin at the earliest ages. Inquiry, invention, and understanding of how things work can begin at the pre-K level.

INVENTORS CORP

We need the formation of an "Inventors Corp" that current inventors and patent holders can join. The purpose of the Corp would be to bring an understanding and appreciation for inventorship to students and to the educational system as a whole. While USPTO has some small programs, this one should be under the purview of the Department of Education. Allowing students to see people like them who are inventors and hear their stories can go a long way to demonstrating that everyone can be an inventor. Specific attention needs to be paid to rural, inner-city, and underserved school districts.

PATENT OFFICE OUTREACH

The USPTO and related agencies should establish additional resource centers that allow the public to learn and potentially access legal, technical, and other advice around the patenting of an invention. While the USPTO has five regional offices, with smaller offices in multiple jurisdictions, the ability for these offices to reach all people who wish to patent and learn about patents is quite limited.

New York City has multiple resource centers and volunteer groups to help inventors, including pro bono groups of lawyers who can help the new inventor. Other states such as Iowa, Wyoming, Utah, and Arizona have no regional center and just one local center for the entire state. The lack of coverage by USPTO is a disadvantage especially for rural and disenfranchised individuals.

All inventors should have access to patent attorneys and/or patent agents who can help secure their intellectual property rights. While it's not essential to have a patent attorney or agent, having one makes the success rate much higher. Here is a place where SBA and the Department of Education should play a role. For example, we should ask the various institutions of higher learning across the country to serve as homes for USPTO resource centers and ask law schools to serve as sources of potential pro bono services for inventors.

MEDICAL UTILITY

The COVID-19 pandemic uncovered great weaknesses in our healthcare system, ranging from disparities in access to healthcare to vulnerabilities, comorbidities, and other conditions, such as multigenerational household living, which make some more vulnerable to COVID-19 and to a higher mortality rate.

Significant research needs to be a priority in order to examine the origins of viral transmission and other important areas of scientific study. The global pandemic placed infectious disease at the forefront of the lives of all U.S. residents. With the likelihood of future pandemics affecting the U.S., new technology and improvements to existing technology need to keep pace. Supply chains, vaccines, treatments, and improved and new types of personal protective equipment (PPE) would all benefit from the patent process and encouraging inventions.

BUSINESS START-UP PACKAGE

Because the timelines for medical innovations are long and the regulatory scrutiny is often time-consuming, investment money is not as present in the ecosystem of start-up biotech. Further access to NIH and other government grants is limited more to existing and well-known theories in health and medicine rather than to more innovative ideas.

A business start-up package to encourage new businesses and technology start-ups, including biotech, to patent early in their life cycles could prove to be an enormous stimulus booster. Giving start-ups (small businesses) a voucher for one to three patent fee waivers for the first three initial filings could supplant the reduced fees for small business entities program that currently exists at the USPTO, and substantially increase the ability for a small business to participate in the patent/intellectual property process.

PATENT REFORM

Patent reform needs to occur so that once inventors are granted patents, the court system does not spend valuable resources, nor inventors spend time and money, having larger corporations invalidate patent rights. Patent infringement is real, and litigation can often resolve cases where infringement is alleged. Especially in the last twenty-five years, the court system has modified laws written by Congress to make exceptions to the laws in very inconsistent and arbitrary ways. The consequence has been to carve away multiple claims, either because a technology could not have been imagined, or appears implausible, or is deemed to be a "law of nature" after those at the USPTO have deemed it to be novel and patentable. An often-cited example of this is the patent for charging stations used for electric cars, which was deemed "abstract" by a Federal Court of Appeals.

The erosion of our patent system by the judiciary needs to be brought back to a place where the playing field is level and the ability for the USPTO to grant patents and or trademarks is solidly covered by the laws that Congress makes.

Without reform in this area, those with lesser means will be at a greater disadvantage in the patent system and will be discouraged from patenting overall. We need to have a system that awards innovation, even in the face of a non-inventor's or non-scientist's determination that the invention is abstract or not feasible.

Federal investment in programs that have broad outreach in education, securing intellectual property rights, and stimulating small businesses can add to the economy at every level and bring the kind of innovation to our country that our Founding Fathers envisioned for us.

Own your talent. Own your contributions. Own your innovations. By doing so, you raise us all up.

> Our forefathers thought highly enough of patents and intellectual property to embed them into the United States Constitution.
>
> Own your talent. Own your contributions. Own your ideas and innovations. By doing so, you raise us all up.

CHAPTER 16
ENGAGE WITH YOUR COMMUNITY

We cannot seek achievement for ourselves and forget about progress and prosperity for our community . . . Our ambitions must be broad enough to include the aspirations and needs of others, for their sakes and for our own.

—CESAR CHAVEZ, LABOR ORGANIZER

In the last few years there have been many articles written about the loss of the front porch in our lives. Some observers such as Miami University professor Elizabeth Plater-Zyberk see the loss of the front porch having to do with cars in driveways producing fumes, and the advent of air-conditioning and television encouraging people to move inside on hot evenings so that porch sitting was no longer advantageous.[54]

If you grew up in a city or even in a nearby city suburb, you likely had a front stoop. Just look around Brooklyn and you see myriad brownstones; many have small platforms at the top of stairs leading from the front door or what is commonly known as a "stoop." I spent part of my childhood in Briarcliff, New York, and part in Yonkers, New York. Our Briarcliff house had a backyard patio, and while one of our Yonkers homes had a front porch, one had a stoop. The patio really allowed only for direct invitational socialization because we had to invite someone into our backyard. The stoop, however, had its own allure, and often people who were passing by or who lived next door or in the neighborhood had an open invitation to sit with us on the stoop. I remember listening to a television interview in the early 1990s during which New Jersey psychologist Ginger Grancagnolo talked about the downfall of our society emanating from the loss of the front stoop.

That stoop on hot summer nights allowed discourse for the adults and for the kids to stay out late and play. Talk about the news of the day would go on every night on the front stoop.

Today kids do not go out and "play." When I was a child we came home from school, changed our clothes, went out, and played. It was unstructured play time with our friends. Today children have "play dates" where they have scheduled time with their friends, and often the play is a structured activity. Kids have sports, music lessons, and a host of other activities, all scheduled, all structured, and free time is lost. A child's engagement with the community and their peers is now changed and is parentally sourced rather than child or individually sourced.

In general, it is true we don't engage in quite the same way nowadays. The sources of community are different—instead of sitting on the front stoop chatting, we might be exchanging comments about a funny cat meme or a cute dog video on Instagram or

Facebook while the kids skirmish in online video games. This is the new face of the individual engagement with community: it lacks a face-to-face aspect, it is not free-form, and it's missing, in many ways, deep engagement in the moment.

The fact that I felt the need to write a chapter about engaging with the community is intriguing and even a little amusing to me. It shows how far we have moved from the days when involvement in your neighborhood, your church, the local amateur theatre company, or a sports club were just part of the fabric of society. You didn't need to be told to do it—it was just what everyone did, in their own way.

Many of us tend to think of community engagement as something we *should* do because it's the right thing and it benefits others. It's a duty, nothing more. I have a slightly different perspective. Outside of my own business I wear a number of other hats: I'm an advisor to The Aspen Institute, I'm a board member for DREAM Charter School in Harlem, and I'm on the board for Springboard Enterprises, just to name a few. These activities benefit others, certainly, but they benefit me too. They are for the common good, and they are for *my* good. By being involved in these organizations I learn about different verticals. I've learned far more about education, about fiduciary responsibility, and about running an organization than I ever would have if I had focused solely on my own business enterprise.

Remember in chapter 2 we spoke about having "vision" and looking around? In a *Harvard Business Review* article, Ken Banta and Orlan Boston discussed what they called the "strategic side gig."[55] Ken Banta is the founder of the Vanguard Network, a leadership-development and networking membership program for high-potential senior leaders, while Orlan Boston is a partner in Ernst & Young's Global Health Sciences practice. From a series of in-depth interviews with private- and public-sector leaders of varying ages and career stages, they distilled some key lessons about the benefits of exploring opportunities in a variety of functions, industries, and geographies outside of your day job. In their view, "Leaders who want to rise—and help their organizations thrive—need to find ways to expand their field of vision and build their knowledge, skills, and connections even as they carry on their daily work." [56]

There is a vast expanse of engagement opportunities to tap into. We're talking everything from board memberships, teaching, fellowships, mentoring, advising, and investing in start-ups to leadership roles in professional associations and clubs and speaking at or organizing idea forums, festivals, and conferences. As Banta and Boston conclude, all of these can be broadly defined as "meaningful engagement in outside activities that expose you to different people, information, and cultures but are also in some way synergistic with both your personal interests and your current or future primary work." [57]

An excellent example of the remarkable yet unforeseen outcomes of such engagement is Amit Paley, who rose from journalist to McKinsey consultant to becoming the CEO of The Trevor Project. Paley spoke to his time as a volunteer at The Trevor Project: "By investing my time outside work in things I was passionate about, I learned things that made me better at my job . . . . Those experiences also prepared me for future leadership roles that I didn't know I would have." [58]

Another example comes from Kara Medoff Barnett, the executive director of the American Ballet Theatre. She's also a member of the advisory committee of the American Theatre Wing, a term member of the Council on Foreign Relations, and a 2015 Henry Crown Fellow of The Aspen Institute. Her filter for selecting the activities to give her time to is simple: "Participate in the ones that spark your intellectual curiosity. Meet people you wouldn't encounter in your current industry or workplace. Open your aperture."[59]

As with all things, there is a balance to be had between enjoying the benefits that community engagement offers you and refraining from being completely self-seeking. "It's incredibly important when you engage in activities outside work that you do it for sincere reasons and not just as a way to self-promote or to rub shoulders with potential professional connections,"[60] says Kathryn Wylde, the president and CEO of the Partnership for New York City, a not-for-profit that focuses on the economy, education, and infrastructure of NYC.

Even the idea of "exposure" can be seen both ways. Here I use the term not in the sense of boosting your own profile and seeking fame, but in the sense of being exposed to fresh perspectives. Others will see it differently, but celebrity has never been that important to me. I don't feel the need to relate to someone other than as another human being. It's maybe paradoxical, then, that I often find myself meeting highly influential and even famous people. Some think of this "exposure" as "networking," but again, I believe that this work is of benefit because of new perspectives and diverse points of view.

Six or seven years ago I was invited to a dinner by Lloyd Blankfein, who was CEO of Goldman Sachs at that time. Afterward I mentioned it to a friend of mine who is a banker on the West Coast.

"You went to that dinner? Who else was there?" she asked.

"I don't know. I mean, I sat next to Steve Case," I replied, mentioning one of America's best-known entrepreneurs and an internet pioneer.

"Oh, wow. Who else did you talk to?"

"Well, there was Bob Wright—I know him from the Autism group." Bob Wright and his late wife, Suzanne, founded Autism Speaks, which is now one of the leading Autism advocacy organizations. Bob also happens to be former president and CEO of NBC. But I know him primarily as a guy I met through my work in Autism.

Another time I was invited to a charity fashion show—the first fashion show I've ever attended. Kim Kardashian was sitting across from me and the room was full of celebrities. Before the show started, I was standing by the red carpet with a couple of younger colleagues, watching people arrive.

"Who's that?" one of them asked, indicating a young woman getting out of a limousine.

"Oh, that's Cardi B," I said.

My colleagues looked at me, clearly wondering how I knew who Cardi B was. I shrugged.

"I played softball with her last week."

We played together at a charity softball event, otherwise I probably wouldn't have had any idea. My team calls me "Forrest Gump" because I have managed to meet so many people along this journey of mine, but it's not something I seek out.

To me, community engagement is the one way to gain many of the attributes we've discussed in this book. As we discussed when looking at vision and the landscape, we have much to learn from the periphery. Here is why community engagement is important:

Use observation to solve problems, as we saw in chapter 1. When discussing leadership, we saw that problem-solving is key to effective leadership. In their groundbreaking article "The Strategic

Side Gig," Ken Banta and Orlan Boston discussed some important leaders and how their involvement in other roles was key to their success in their main field. For example, they cite former chairman and CEO of Allergan, David Pyott, who served on many boards outside the pharmaceutical industry during his career. He says the extra roles he took on helped him meet potential commercial partners, identify trends, and understand prospective markets. "You realize how different the world looks from the other side," [61] he explains.

Thinking broadly is a core attribute of a good leader, as we also saw in chapter 1. "As the business world becomes more complex, it's increasingly difficult to find solutions in a single field or discipline," says Mehmood Khan, former CSO at Pepsi. "You can do a lot on your own time, such as helping nonprofits in the community where you live," he says. "Look for these opportunities. Every experience can be a value-add." [62]

Have a wider vision, which we talked about in chapter 2. Ken Mehlman is the global head of public affairs and cohead of global impact at the investment firm KKR and a fellow trustee and friend at F&M. He says, "Lateral thinking beats linear thinking every day of the week," he says. "What's critical these days is to bring a different perspective and apply it to whatever you're doing. And you can't do that if all your attention and focus is limited to the four walls of your organization." [63]

Appreciate the many forms that innovation takes by looking outside the status quo, as chapter 9 examined. When you do important work in other fields, your understanding is expanded, and you make connections that enable you to be a better leader.

Personal growth occurs through flexibility, the willingness to step outside your comfort zone, as we saw in chapter 12. Mehmood

Khan says, "To develop as a leader, you need to leave your comfort zone. That's how personal growth occurs." [64]

Empathy requires us to see the world as others see it, as we explored in chapters 1 and 15. Former chairman and CEO of Docusign Keith Krach says of his mentoring work, "It broadens my scope of empathy and understanding. As my mom always told me, the best way to learn is through OPE: other people's experiences." [65]

In many books I find that the last chapter is the cherry on the cake, a pleasing add-on to the main event. But I believe that this chapter on community engagement *is* the main event, bringing together every principle we have walked through in the preceding pages. By engaging with the world around us and stepping outside our familiar space, we build so many of the qualities that enable us to overcome obstacles on our way to changing the world.

> By engaging with the world around us and stepping outside of our familiar space, we build so many of the qualities that enable us to overcome obstacles on our way to changing the world.

CONCLUSION

BECOMING A
THOUGHT LEADER

Leadership and learning are indispensable to each other.
—JOHN F. KENNEDY, PRESIDENT OF THE UNITED STATES 1961–1963

Through these remarkable years I have spent as an entrepreneur, I have learned that leadership is essential and essentially is a simple concept. Good leaders solve problems; bad leaders think of themselves.

We have seen throughout these pages that entrepreneurship, changemaking, and leadership, including thought leadership and personal growth, are deeply intertwined. They need to be approached in concert.

Just as political leaders have a mandate to make the lives of their constituents better and to represent their views, I believe that business leaders have a responsibility to solve problems, both in what they do for their customers and in the wider world, and in how they conduct their internal business and take care of their employees.

During the COVID-19 pandemic, many political leaders were more concerned about their own futures than taking care of their constituents, some of whom were out of work and even hungry. Set against such inaction and self-interest, business leaders were pivoting fast to keep their companies going while many were also trying to solve the problems of their community at large. Restaurants were trying to stay alive while feeding those who suffered from food insecurity. The best of them solved problems through innovation, inventing new ways to do business. Wayfair, the online furniture and home goods company, is an example of this. In March 2020 when the pandemic hit, they pivoted fast to implement new social distancing practices in their warehouses and a new system of shifts so there was no overlap of employees. These were necessary measures to keep the business afloat, but what is remarkable and perhaps counterintuitive is that Wayfair also raised its workers' rate of pay. They brought in a dinners-to-go program so that twice a week everyone who worked in one of their warehouses could take home a meal for their whole family. Not only did that help their own workers, it bolstered the local independent restaurants near their locations that were being hard-hit by the pandemic. These were very smart moves. As people were asked to shelter in place during the worst times of the pandemic and children were relegated to online homeschooling, Wayfair knew that its business would likely increase as people's homes became the nexus of their lives. They would need a stable employee base. By feeding their employees and giving them raises, the company bolstered their team against loss of income from a spouse or other difficulties their employees might have faced during this challenging time.

Acts of kindness and compassion are very often the best possible business strategy.

Remember that leadership requires seeking out real problems to solve and empowering those whom you lead on every level to help accomplish your task. Surround yourself with diverse viewpoints and listen to them. Be an example and take care of those around you.

The insights into leadership that I have gained along my own path to innovation are applicable for all entrepreneurs, but especially for women and others who have historically been marginalized in the corporate world.

Let the precepts in this book—observing widely, seeking talent, innovating in the spaces between, applying logic, blocking out the noise, bending without breaking, taking ownership, believing in yourself, being engaged, and most importantly, being empathetic—become your entrepreneur mantra. With them, you will be the kind of leader who solves problems and changes the world. Engage by sharing what you have learned with the greater community. There is no value in learning what you have without sharing the greatness and goodness you have found in your journey.

ACKNOWLEDGMENTS

This book would not exist without the help of the amazing Sally Collings. Her writing, editorial, and creative skills helped bring my ideas and writings to life.

To my family—Jay, Kathy, and James—you always have my back and have figured out how to navigate life with me. While dedicated to helping children, my life often manages to take precedence over everything else. Thank you for the indulgence.

My deepest thanks to:
- My Curemark family
- My dear family in California
- The Skai Blue Media family
- My Springboard family
- My DREAM family
- My VRL family
- My PitCCh In family
- My trustee families at F&M and PRATT
- My Yankees family
- My book support team—Janice, Jason, and Anne
- The team at Forefront Books

- All the children, including James and Jamie, who have touched my life
- My friends, Ken, Ann, Stacy, Greg, Vanessa, Joanna, and all of you who all continually are a part of my everyday life and are family to me

Thank you because
    Change Is Hard
    Change Is Scary
    Change Is Necessary
    Change Necessitates Embracing Uncertainty
    Change Involves Risk
    Change Requires Self-Examination
    Change Needs Encouragement
    Change Needs Love

Without all of you, none of this change would be.

ENDNOTES

1   d.school, https://dschool.stanford.edu/about.
2   Brené Brown, *I Thought It Was Just Me (but it isn't)* (Avery, 2007).
3   Kansas State University website, https://www.k- state.edu/ psych/ research/loschkylester.html.
4   Adam Larson and Lester Loschky, "The contributions of central versus peripheral vision to scene gist recognition," *Journal of Vision9*, no. 6 (September 2009), https://jov.arvojournals.org/ article.aspx?articleid=2122327.
5   Daniel Kalberer, "Peripheral Awareness and Visual Reaction Time in Professional Football Players in the National Football League," *Optometry and Visual Performance5*, no. 4 (August 2017), https://www. ovpjournal.org/ uploads/ 2/ 3/ 8/ 9/ 23898265/ ovp5- 4_article_kalberer_ web.pdf.
6   "Why Business Leaders Should Solve Problems Beyond Their Companies." HBR Ideacast, Episode 719.
7   Robert Kormoczi, "Most Powerful Companies," Times International, May 14, 2020, https://timesinternational.net/ what- is- the- most- powerful-company/.
8   BRAC, http://www.brac.net/partnership.
9   Image adapted from https://hbr.org/2020/05/begin-with-trust.
10 Josh Wyner and Martin Kurzweil, "Invest in Talent to Move the Dial on Socioeconomic Diversity on Nation's College Campuses," Aspen

Institute, March 2, 2018, https://www.aspeninstitute.org/blog-posts/ invest- talent- move- dial- socioeconomic- diversity- nations- college- campuses/.

11 "Mixed backgrounds improve organizational innovation, creativity." *Michigan News*, June 25, 2008, https://news.umich.edu/ mixed- back- grounds-improve-organizational-innovation-creativity/.

12 Abby Budiman et al., "Facts on U.S. immigrants, 2018," Pew Research Center, August 20, 2020, https://www.pewresearch.org/ hispanic/ 2020/08/20/facts-on-u-s-immigrants/.

13 Leilah Janah, https://www.leilajanah.com/.

14 Daniel R. Porterfield, "In America, Talent Must Rise," Aspen Insti- tute, June 5, 2018, https://www.aspeninstitute.org/ of- interest/ in- america-talent-must-rise/.

15 Candice Georgiadis, "Dr. Joan Fallon of Curemark: 5 Things I Wish Someone Told Me Before I Became A CEO," *Authority Magazine*, January 10, 2020, https://medium.com/ authority- magazine/ dr- joan- fallon- of- curemark- 5- things- i- wish- someone- told- me- before- i- became-a-ceo-890cb7b2581e.

16 Dawn Papandrea, "Career experts share how long you should stay at a job — and how to explain 'job-hopping' to a potential employer," *Business Insider*, May 11, 2018, https://www.businessinsider.com/career- experts-share-how-long-you-should-stay-at-a-job-2018-5.

17 Fifth Sense, https://www.fifthsense.org.uk/psychology-and-smell/.

18 Marlene Maheu, Pamela Whitten, and Ace Allen, *E-Health, Telehealth, and Telemedicine: A Guide to Startup and Success* (John Wiley & Sons, 2002).

19 Aaron Holmes, "Video- conferencing apps were downloaded an unprecedented 62 million times last week, reflecting a new normal in how people interact," *Business Insider*, March 31, 2020, https://www. businessinsider.com/video-conferencing-apps-62-million-downloads- zoom-houseparty-hangouts-teams-2020-3.

20 Hans Halvorson, *How Logic Works: A User's Guide* (Princeton Univer- sity Press, 2020).

21 Ellie Murphy, "What are the common errors or bias within induc- tive/deductive reasoning?" ResearchGate, April 17, 2015, https:// www.researchgate.net/post/ What_are_the_common_errors_ or_bias_

within_inductive_deductive_reasoning.

22 Daniel Miessler, "The Difference Between Deductive and Inductive Reasoning," Daniel Miessler, September 23, 2020, https://danielmiessler.com/blog/the-difference-between-deductive-and-inductive-reasoning/.

23 Alissa Walker, "Google Patented a Sticky Car Hood That Traps Pedestrians Like Flies," Gizmodo, May 18, 2016, https://gizmodo.com/google-patented-a-sticky-car-hood-that-traps-pedestrian-1777376162.

24 Alissa Walker, "Google Patented a Sticky Car Hood That Traps Pedestrians Like Flies."

25 Alissa Walker, "Google Patented a Sticky Car Hood That Traps Pedestrians Like Flies."

26 Jeremey Donovan, *How to Deliver a TED Talk* (McGraw-Hill Education, 2013).

27 Jimmy Whitworth, "Coronavirus: Why Testing and Contact Tracing Isn't a Simple Solution," *The Conversation*, April 30, 2020.

28 George Leigh Mallory quote, Quote Master, https://www.quotemaster.org/q4c4d1c06f0bde929c9e4fdaecb6bcdfd.

29 Emily Bazelon, "How Do We Contend With Trump's Defiance of 'Norms'?" *The New York Times*, July 11, 2017, https://www.nytimes.com/2017/07/11/magazine/how-do-we-contend-with-trumps-defiance-of-norms.html.

30 Sharon Begley, "Trump Said More Covid-19 Testing 'Creates More Cases.' We Did the Math," *STAT*, July 20, 2020, https://www.statnews.com/2020/07/20/trump-said-more-covid19-testing-creates-more-cases-we-did-the-math/.

31 Dan Sabbagh, "'Wishful thinking': the dangers of UK hype during Covid-19," *The Guardian*, August 7, 2020, https://www.theguardian.com/world/2020/aug/07/wishful-thinking-the-dangers-of-uk-hype-during-covid-19.

32 Alsin Goerge, "What Gamblers and Weather Forecasters Can Teach Us About Risk," *Slate*, May 22, 2012, https://slate.com/technology/2012/05/risk-intelligence-how-gamblers-and-weather-forecasters-assess-probabilities.html.

33 Ibid.

34 Samantha Smithstein, "Facebook, Privacy, and Personal Responsibility,"

Psychology Today, May 21, 2010, https://www.psychologytoday.com/us/blog/what-the-wild-things-are/201005/facebook-privacy-and-personal-responsibility.

35 Andrew Beaton, "Decoding an Outbreak: How Covid-19 Ripped through the Baltimore Ravens," *The Wall Street Journal,* December 11, 2020, https://www.wsj.com/articles/decoding-an-outbreak-how-covid-19-ripped-through-the-baltimore-ravens-11607695552.

36 "With great power comes great responsibility," Quote Investigator, https://quoteinvestigator.com/2015/07/23/great-power/.

37 Meredith Somers, "3 ways leaders can make Black lives matter in the workplace," MIT Management, October 8, 2020, https://mitsloan.mit.edu/ideas-made-to-matter/3-ways-leaders-can-make-black-lives-matter-workplace.

38 Darrell K. Rigby, Sarah Elk, and Steve Berez, "Start Stopping Faster," *Harvard Business Review,* September 22, 2020, https://hbr.org/2020/09/start-stopping-faster.

39 David Sheinin, "Velocity is Strangling Baseball—And Its Grip Keeps Tightening," *The Washington Post,* May 21, 2019, https://www.washingtonpost.com/sports/2019/05/21/velocity-is-strangling-baseball-its-grip-keeps-tightening/.

40 "Thatcher and Queen Elizabeth II: what was their relationship like?" History Extra, BBC History, November 16, 2020, https://www.historyextra.com/period/20th-century/queen-elizabeth-ii-margaret-thatcher-relationship-prime-minister-disagree-friends-crown-netflix/.

41 Dr Ursula M. Wilder, "The Psychology of Espionage," *Studies in Intelligence* 61, no. 2 (Extracts, June 2017), https://www.hsdl.org/?abstract&did=803671.

42 Michael J. Breus, "Better Sleep with 5-HTP," *Psychology Today,* October 12, 2017, https://www.psychologytoday.com/us/blog/sleep-newzzz/201710/better-sleep-5-htp.

43 Kevin Labar, "How Anxiety is Contagious," World Economic Forum, November 12, 2014, https://www.weforum.org/agenda/2014/11/how-anxiety-is-contagious/.

44 "Breaking the Cycle of Shame & Self-Destructive Behavior," Psych

Central, https://psychcentral.com/lib/breaking- the- cycle- of-shame-and-self-destructive-behavior.

45 Brené Brown, "The Power of Vulnerability" TED Talk, Jan 3, 2011, https://www.youtube.com/watch?v=iCvmsMzlF7o.

46 "Narcissistic personality disorder," Mayo Clinic, https://www.mayoclinic.org/ diseases- conditions/ narcissistic- personality- disorder/ symptoms- causes/ syc- 20366662#:~:text=Overview,lack%20of%20empathy%20for%20others.

47 "Employing Innovation Across America." Global Innovation Policy Center December 1, 2015, https://www.theglobalipcenter.com/employing-innovation-across-america-2/.

48 Jennifer Hunt et al, "Why Are Women Underrepresented Amongst Patentees?" *Research Policy* May 2013.

49 Eoin O'Carroll, "Equity pending: Why so few women receive patents," *The Christian Science Monitor*, July 2, 2018, https://www.csmonitor.com/Technology/2018/0702/Equity-pending-Why-so-few-women-receive-patents.

50 Jennifer Hunt, et al, "Why Don't Women Patent?" National Bureau of Economic Research, working paper, March 1, 2012, https://www.nber.org/papers/w17888.

51 Jennifer Hunt et al, "Why Don't Women Patent?"

52 Lindquist M. J. Sol and M. Van Praag (2015) "Why Do Entrepreneurial Parents Have Entrepreneurial Children?" *Journal of Labor Economics* 33, no. 2,, 269- 296, https://econpapers.repec.org/ article/ ucpjlabec/ doi_3a10.1086_2f678493.htm.

53 Jonathan Rothwell, et al, "Patenting Prosperity: Invention and Economic Performance in the United States and its Metropolitan Areas," The Brookings Institution, February 2013, https://www.brookings.edu/ research/ patenting- prosperity- invention- and- economic- performance-in-the-united-states-and-its-metropolitan-areas/.

54 Adrienne Gaffney, "The Rise and Fall of the Front Porch," *The Wall Street Journal*, September 11, 2019, https://www.wsj.com/ articles/ the-rise-and-fall-of-the-front-porch-11568206837.

55 Ken Banta and Orlan Boston, "The Strategic Side Gig," *Harvard Business Review*, May- June 2020, https://hbr.org/ 2020/ 05/ the- strategic-side-gig.

56 Ken Banta and Orlan Boston, "The Strategic Side Gig."

57 Ken Banta and Orlan Boston, "The Strategic Side Gig."

58 Ken Banta and Orlan Boston, "The Strategic Side Gig."

59 Ken Banta and Orlan Boston, "The Strategic Side Gig."

60 Ken Banta and Orlan Boston, "The Strategic Side Gig."

61 Ken Banta and Orlan Boston, "The Strategic Side Gig."

62 Ken Banta and Orlan Boston, "The Strategic Side Gig."

63 Ken Banta and Orlan Boston, "The Strategic Side Gig."

64 Ken Banta and Orlan Boston, "The Strategic Side Gig."

65 Ken Banta and Orlan Boston, "The Strategic Side Gig."